Origami K

32 Projects designed by young folders

Compiled and diagrammed by J.C. Nolan

This book is dedicated with deep gratitude to Richard Alexander and Michael LaFosse of origamido.com – exquisite artisans and dear friends who have dedicated their lives to the promotion and uplifting of origami as an art form.

About this Book

The "Origami Kids" series is dedicated to inspiring youthful folders to design and document models of their own. Contained within this book are 30 wonderful projects created by young folders just like you – some who were simply experimenting and came upon an exciting new creation and some who are serious designers who went on to become recognized names in the origami community.

OrigamiUSA is always looking for new designs from young creators. If in your explorations you come upon a model which you'd like to be considered for Origami by Children you can find submission information at the back of this book or learn more on the web at **www.origamiusa.org/obc.**

All proceeds for "Origami Kids" are donated to OrigamiUSA and "Origami by Children" to foster creativity and exploration in young designers and folders.

Special thanks go out to Michael LaFosse at **origamido.com**, Jeremy Shafer at **www.jeremyevents.com**, Marc Kirschenbaum at **marckrsh.home.pipeline.com**.

This book was created using Adobe Studio CS6 under Windows 7. Fonts used include *Signika* by Anna Giedryś at **ancymonic.com** and *SketchFlow Print.* Cover design by Magda Barker at **magdabarker.com** with assistance by Willie Azali at **www.wazaliart.com.**

Additional information on origami design and other works by J.C. Nolan can be found at **creatingorigami.com** or **lapinpublishing.com.**

Table of Contents

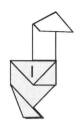

Baby Bald Eagle
Page 13

Flower Arrangement
Page 14

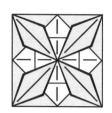

Decoration
Page 15

Simple Ladybug
Page 16

Alfred Hitchcock
Page 18

Jester
Page 20

Heart Stick-pin
Page 23

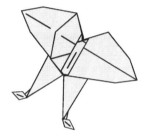

Luna Moth
Page 24

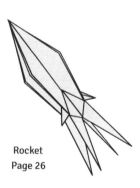

Rocket
Page 26

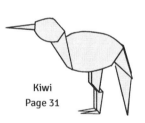

Mother Swan and Two Cygnets
Page 28

Kiwi
Page 31

Multi-form Star
Page 33

Eric's Dragon
Page 35

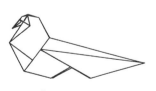

Dove
Page 37

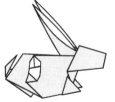

Spotted Bunny
Page 39

Manatee
Page 42

8

Perching Hawk
Page 44

Penguin
Page 48

lower Boxes
Page 52

Screaming Michael
Page 56

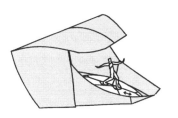

Surfer on a Wave
Page 59

Balloon Man
Page 62

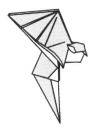

Flapping Bat
Page 64

Weasel
Page 66

White Ibis
Page 69

Heron
Page 72

Opossum
Page 75

Pot-bellied Pig
Page 78

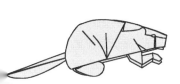

Beaver
Page 82

Folding the Preliminary Base
Page 86

Folding the Blintz Base
Page 88

Rearing Dragon
Page 92

9

Notation and Techniques

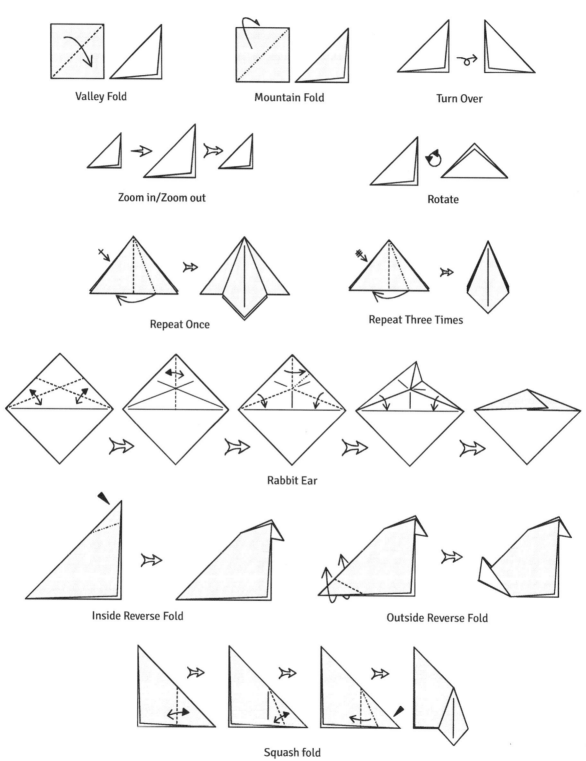

Valley Fold

Mountain Fold

Turn Over

Zoom in/Zoom out

Rotate

Repeat Once

Repeat Three Times

Rabbit Ear

Inside Reverse Fold

Outside Reverse Fold

Squash fold

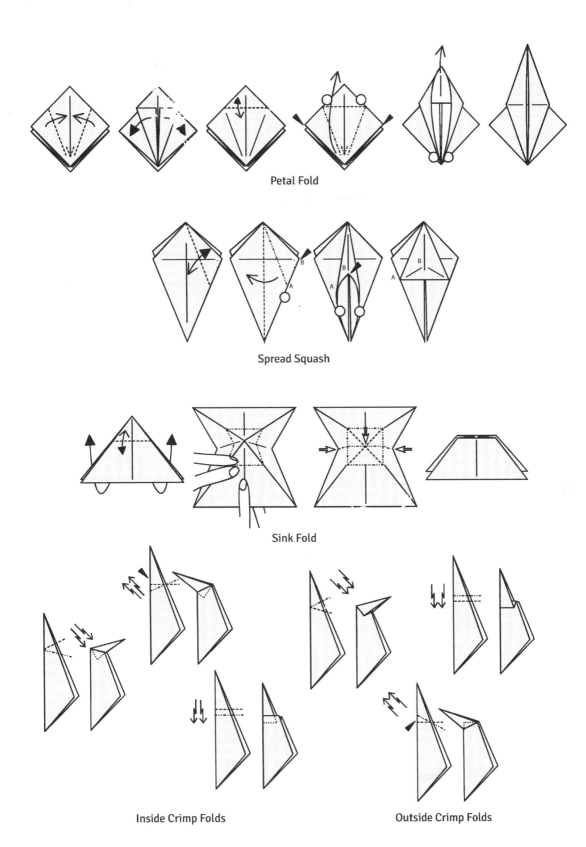

Petal Fold

Spread Squash

Sink Fold

Inside Crimp Folds

Outside Crimp Folds

Baby Bald Eagle

by Julia Ko
Age 8, Level 1

1.

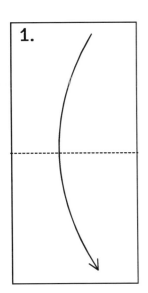

Fold from a 2x1 rectangle of paper, grey on one side, white on the other.
This model was originally designed to be folded from a Canadian $2 bill.

2.

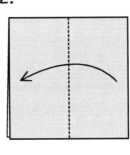

3.

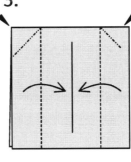

4.

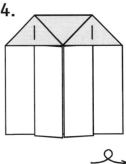

5.

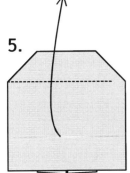

6.

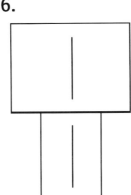

7.

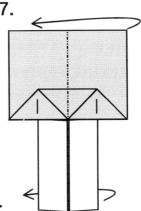

8.

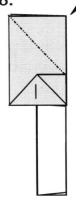

9.

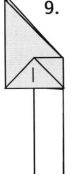

10.

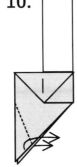

11.

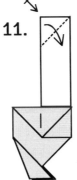

12.

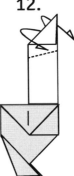

13.

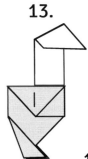

13

Flower Arrangement

by Troy Elliott
Age 12, Level 1

1.

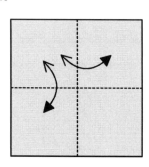

2.

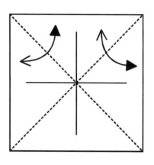

3.

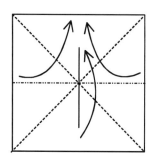

4.

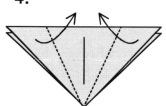

5.

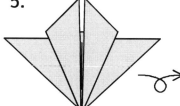

6.

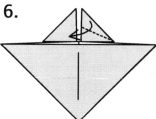

7.

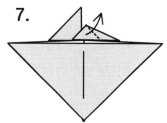

8.

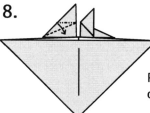

Repeat steps 6-7
on the other side.

9.

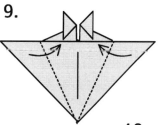

10.

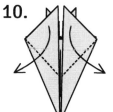

11.

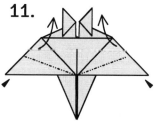

12.

13.

Decoration

by J.C. Nolan
Age 9, Level 1+

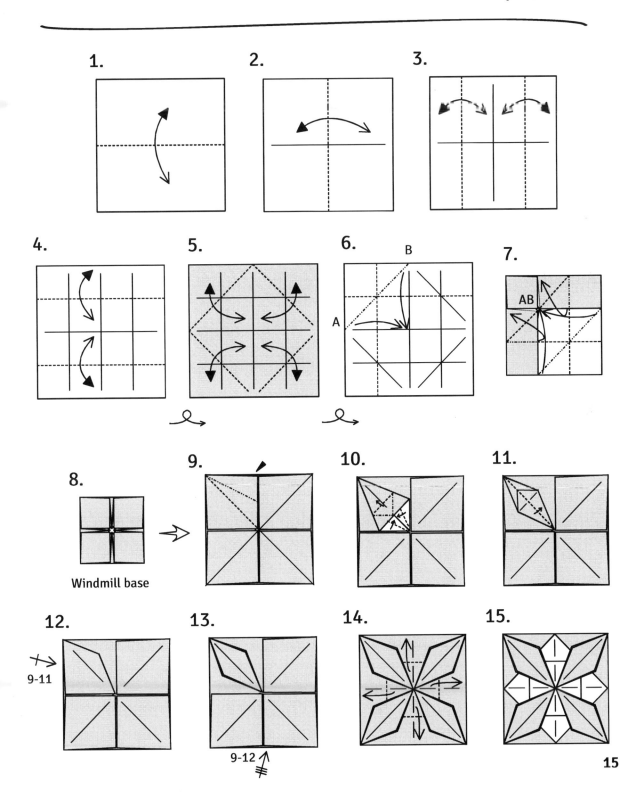

8. Windmill base

15

Ladybug (pureland)

by Aaron Einbond
Age 17, Level 1

1.

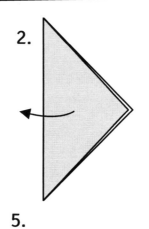

2.

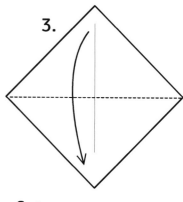

3.

4.

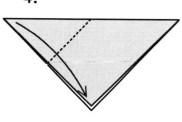

5.

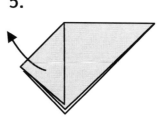

6.

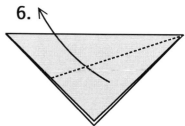

7.

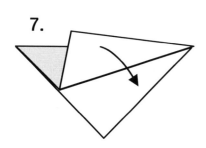

8.

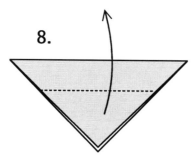

9.

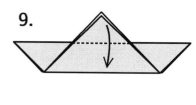

10.

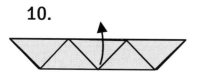

11.

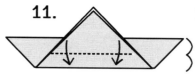

12.

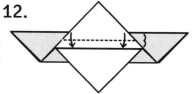

13.

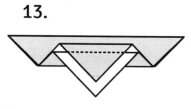

14.

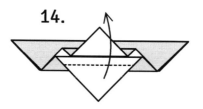

15.

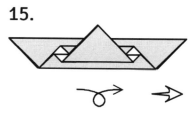

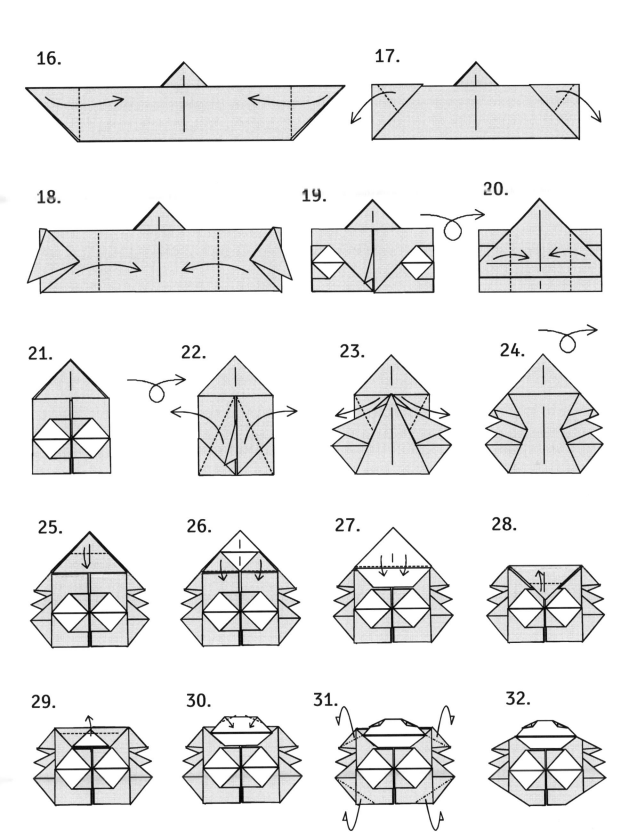

16.

17.

18.

19.

20.

21.

22.

23.

24.

25.

26.

27.

28.

29.

30.

31.

32.

Alfred Hitchcock

by Michael Adcock
Age 14, Level 1+

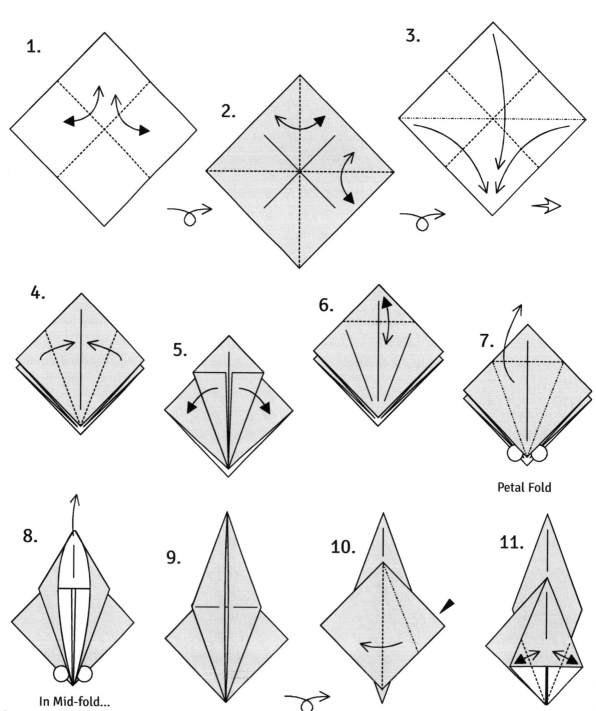

1.

2.

3.

4.

5.

6.

7.

Petal Fold

8.

In Mid-fold...

9.

10.

11.

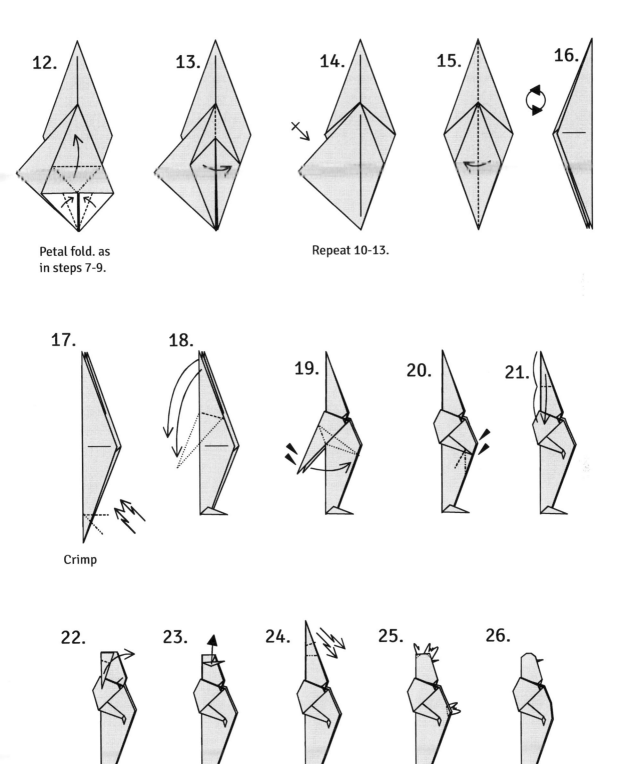

12. Petal fold. as in steps 7-9.

13.

14. Repeat 10-13.

15.

16.

17. Crimp

18.

19.

20.

21.

22.

23.

24.

25.

26.

Jester

by Michael Adcock
Age 14, Level

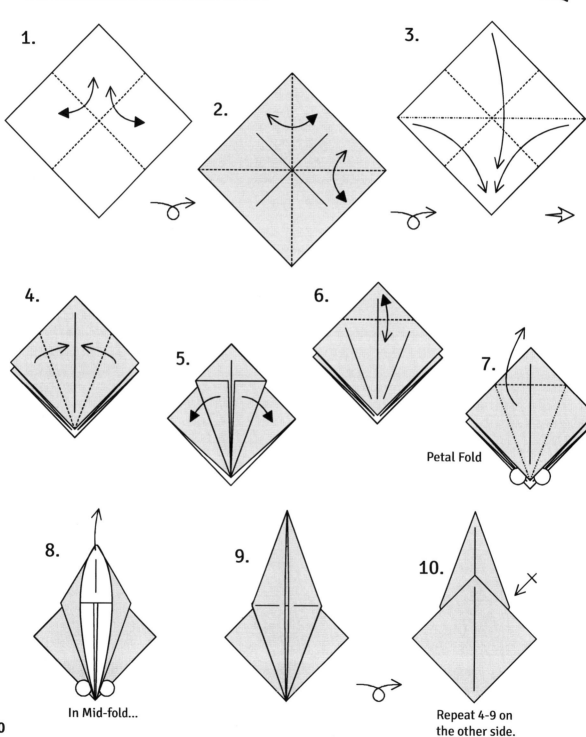

1.

2.

3.

4.

5.

6.

7.

Petal Fold

8.

In Mid-fold...

9.

10.

Repeat 4-9 on
the other side.

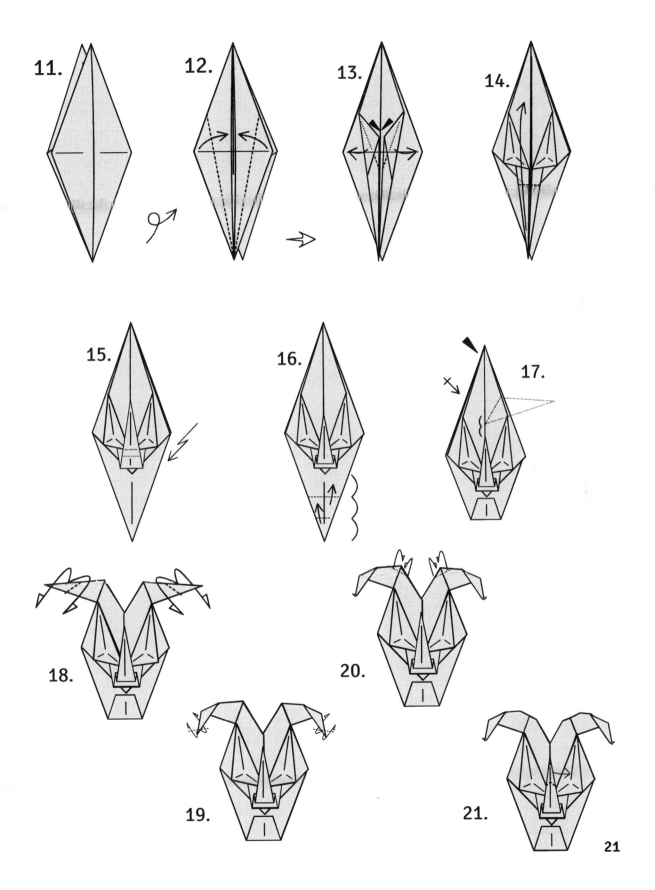

21

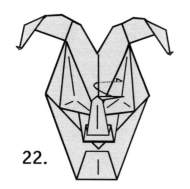

22.

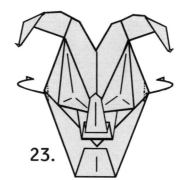

23.

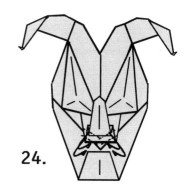

24.

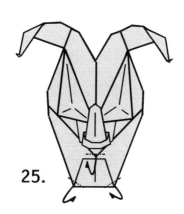

25.

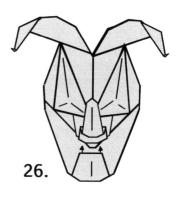

26.

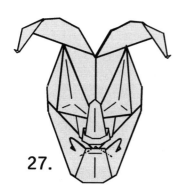

27.

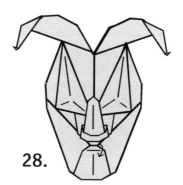

28.

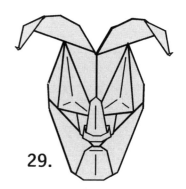

29.

Heart Stick Pin

by Daniel Stillman
Age 16, Level 1+

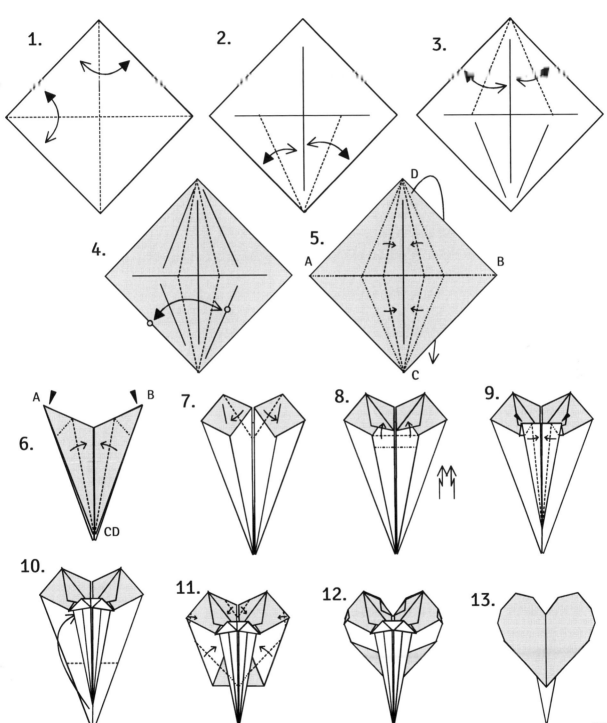

Luna Moth

by Kevin Thorne
Age 17, Level 1+

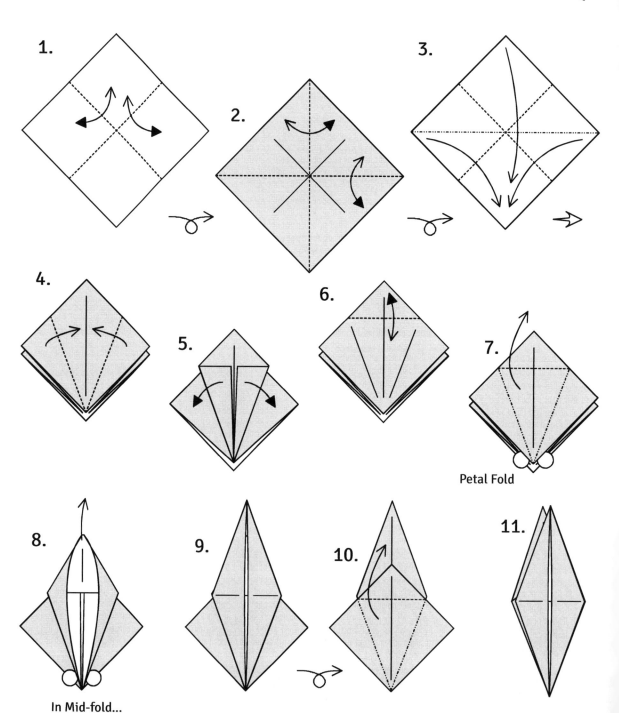

1.

2.

3.

4.

5.

6.

7.

Petal Fold

8.

In Mid-fold...

9.

10.

11.

Repeat 4-9 on the other side.

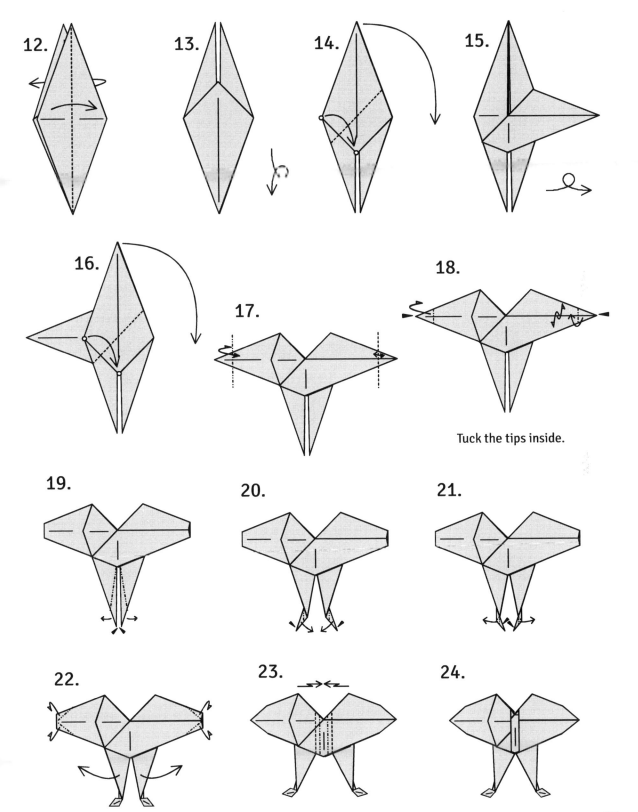

12.

13.

14.

15.

16.

17.

18.

Tuck the tips inside.

19.

20.

21.

22.

23.

24.

25

Rocket

by Kevin Thorne
Age 18, Level 1+

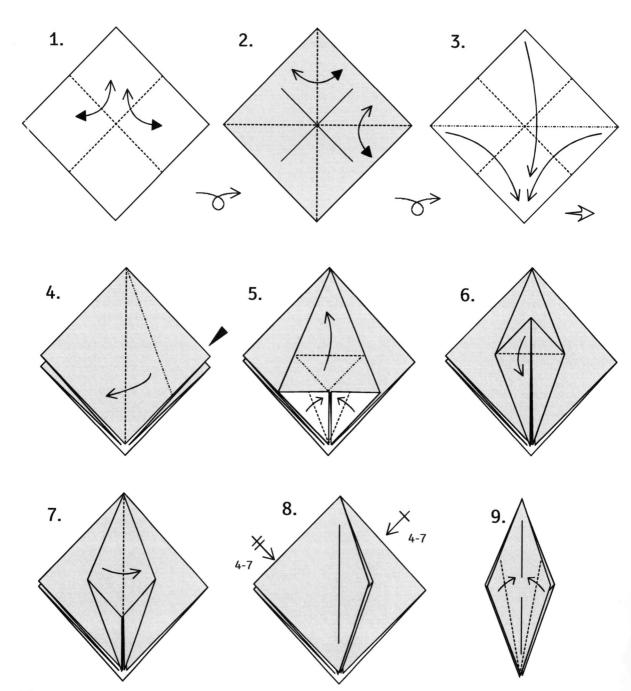

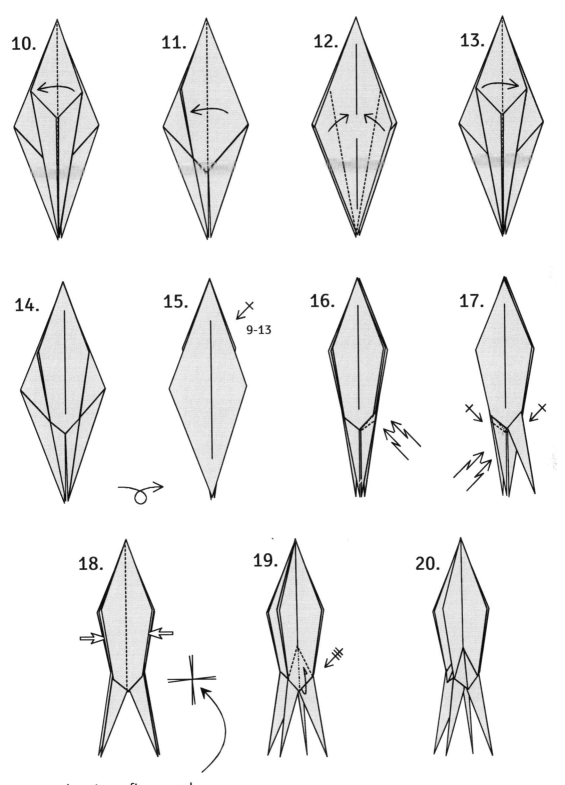

10.

11.

12.

13.

14.

15.

9-13

16.

17.

18.

Insert your fingers and
fan the layers like this.

19.

20.

Mother Swan and Two Cygnets

by Aaron Einbond
Age 9, Level II

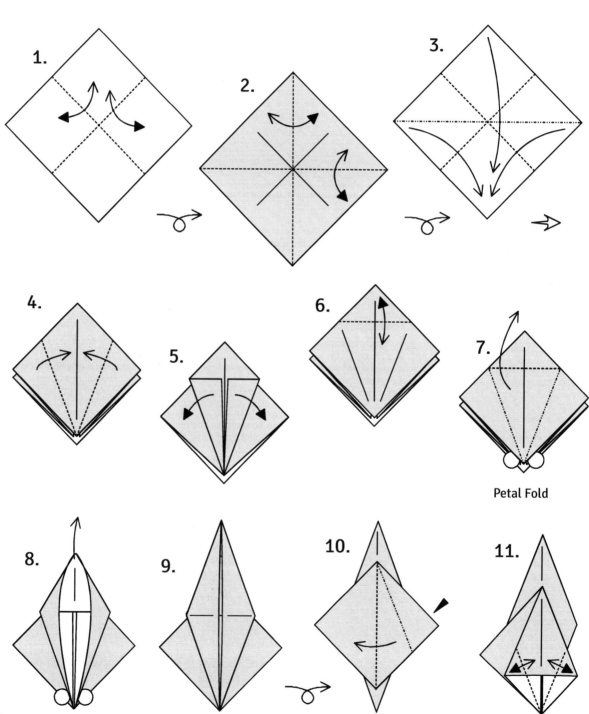

7. Petal Fold

8. In Mid-fold...

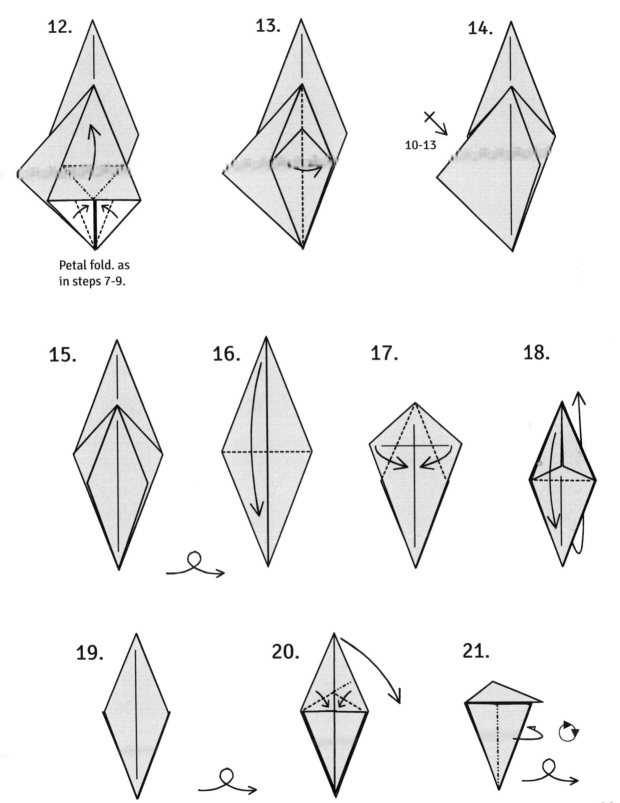

12.

Petal fold. as
in steps 7-9.

13.

14.

10-13

15.

16.

17.

18.

19.

20.

21.

29

22.

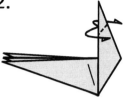

23.

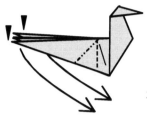

Squash fold the wings.
Note the landmark.

24.

25.

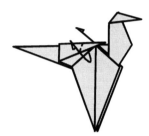

26.

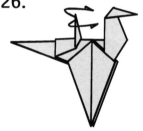

Repeat steps 25-28
on the other flap.

27.

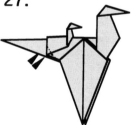

28.

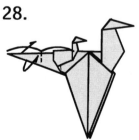

29.

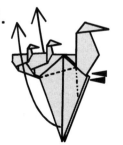

30.

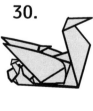

Complete the model with
an unusual petal fold.
The model will become 3D.

Kiwi

by Eric Anderson
Age 11, Level II+

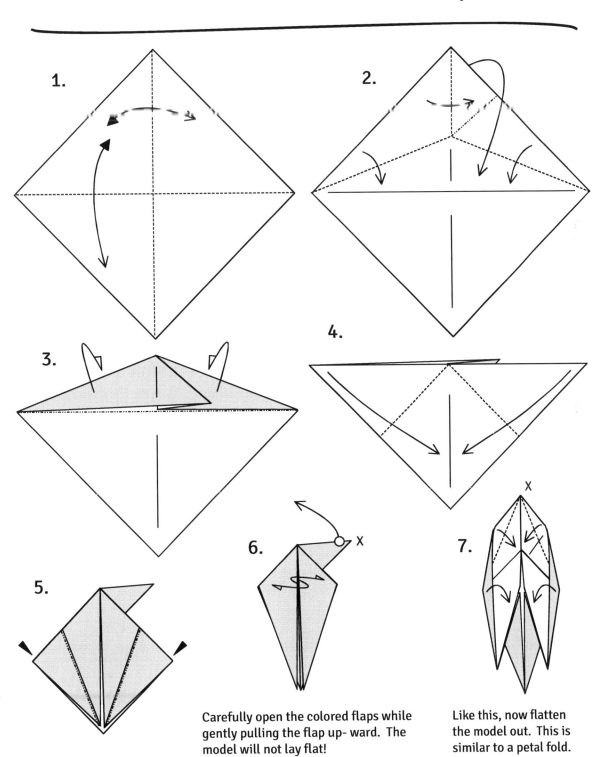

1.

2.

3.

4.

5.

6.

Carefully open the colored flaps while gently pulling the flap up- ward. The model will not lay flat!

7.

Like this, now flatten the model out. This is similar to a petal fold.

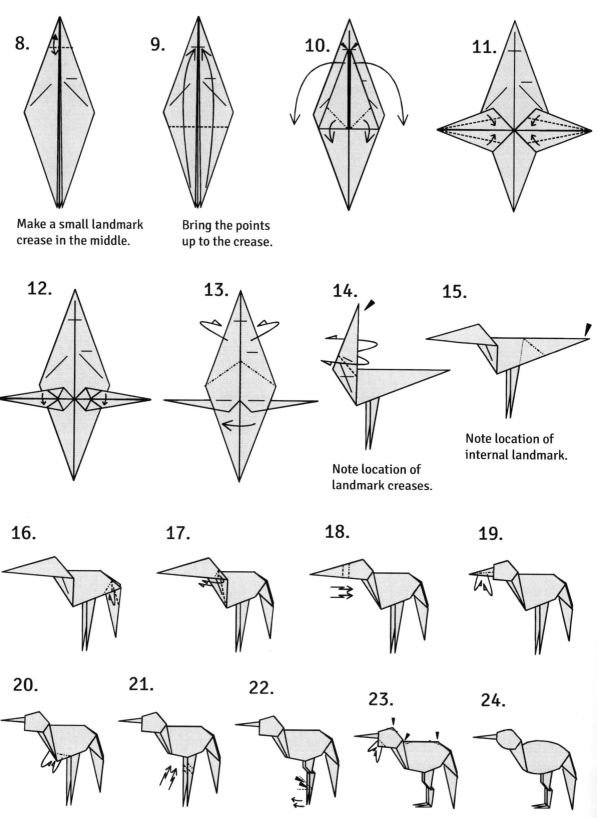

8. Make a small landmark crease in the middle.

9. Bring the points up to the crease.

10.

11.

12.

13.

14. Note location of landmark creases.

15. Note location of internal landmark.

16.

17.

18.

19.

20.

21.

22.

23.

24.

4 Pointed, Multi-form Star

by Daniel E. Moraseski
Age 12, Level II

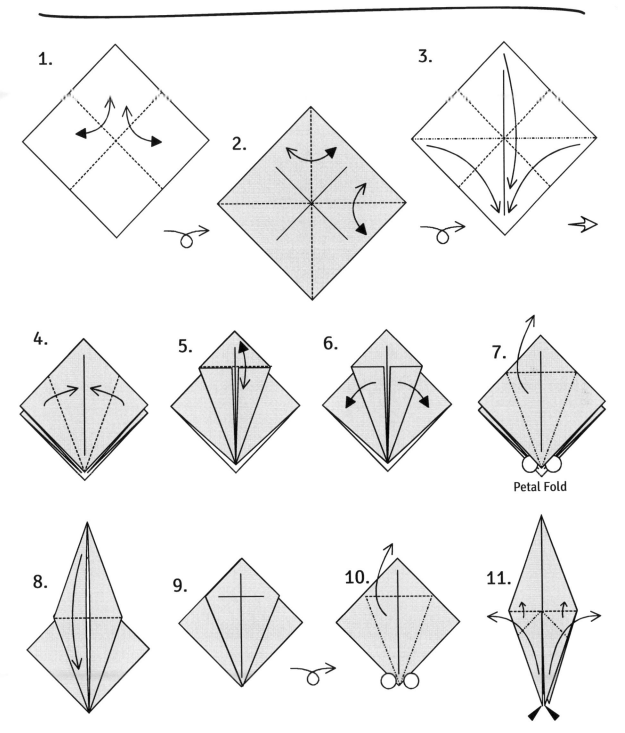

7. Petal Fold

11. Squash fold

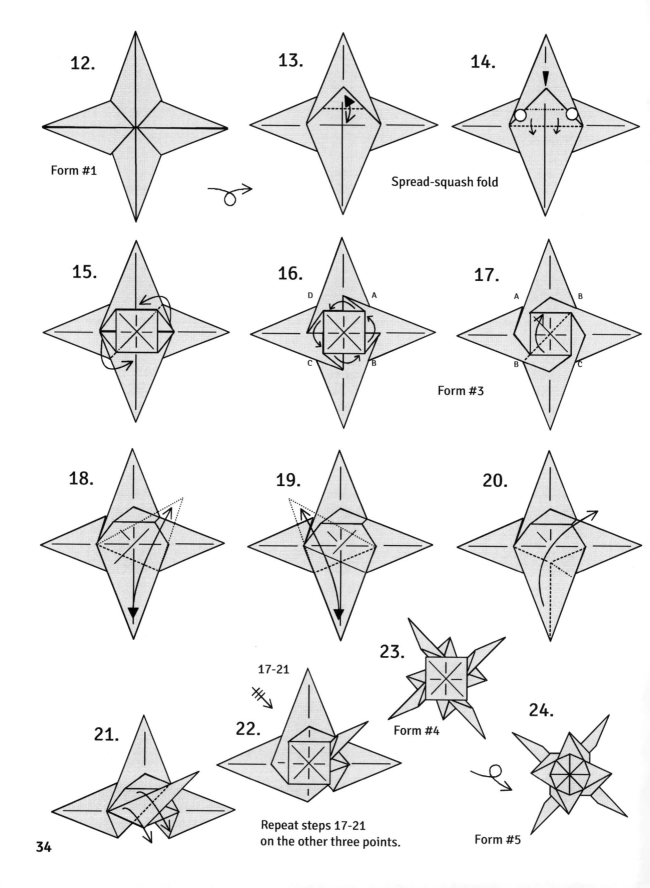

12.

Form #1

13.

14.

Spread-squash fold

15.

16.

17.

Form #3

18.

19.

20.

21.

22.

17-21

Repeat steps 17-21
on the other three points.

23.

Form #4

24.

Form #5

34

Eric's Dragon

by Eric Barr
Age 16, Level II

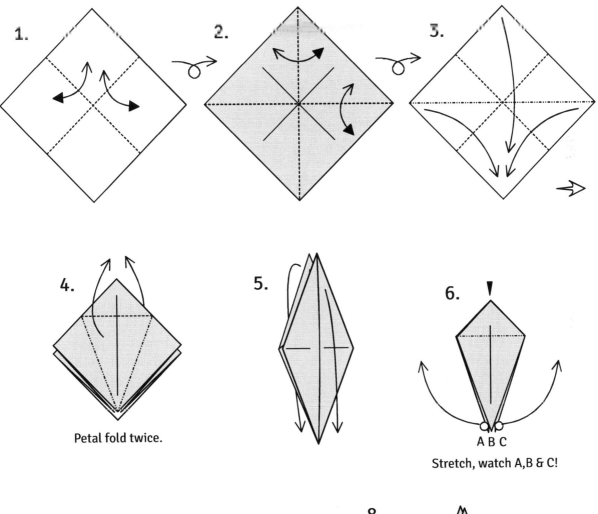

4. Petal fold twice.

6. A B C
Stretch, watch A,B & C!

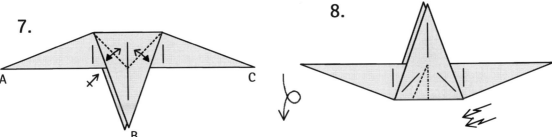

7. A C B

8. Crimp. The model will not lie flat.

9.

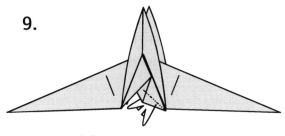

Tuck flaps inside on both sides.

10.

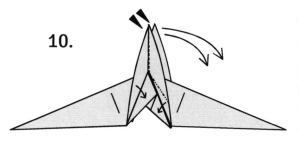

11.

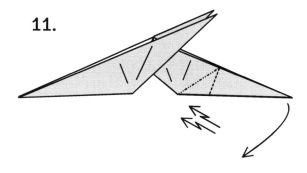

12.

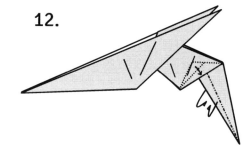

13.

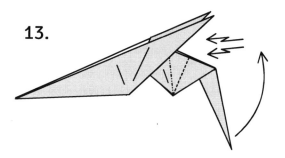

14.

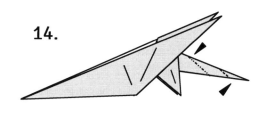

15.

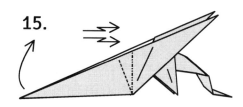

16.

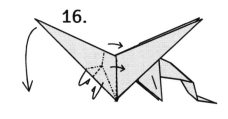

This step is a little tricky...
a double rabbit ear combined
with an outside reverse fold.

17.

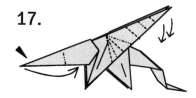

18.

36

Dove

by Michael LaFosse
Age 12, Level II

1.
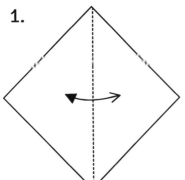

2.
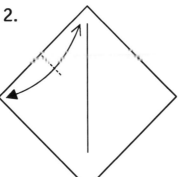

3.
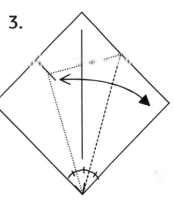

4.
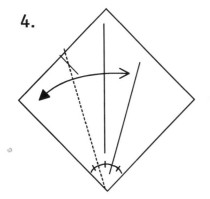

5.
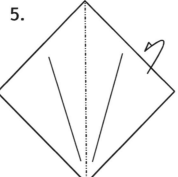

6.
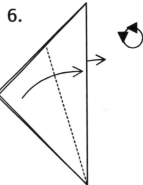

7.
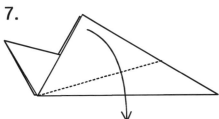

8.
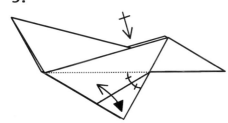

9.
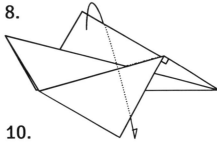

10.
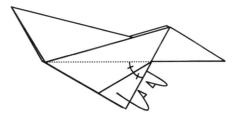

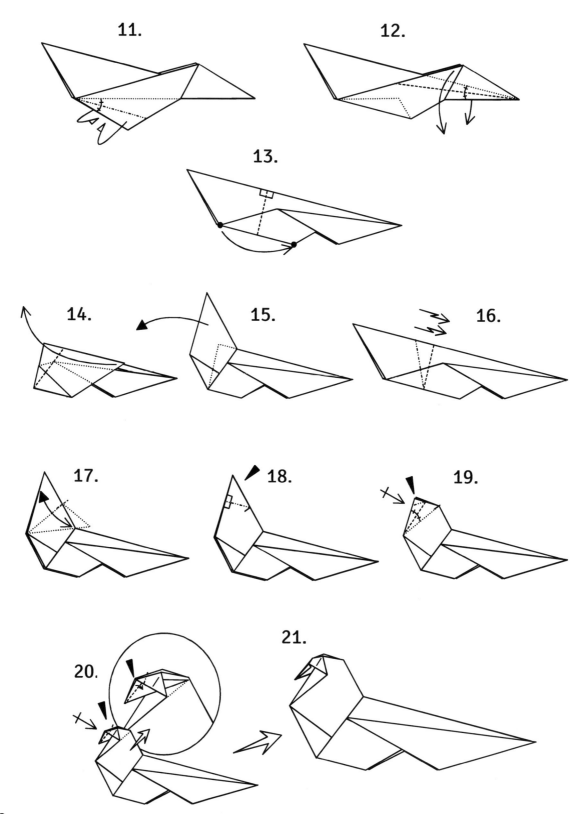

11.

12.

13.

14.

15.

16.

17.

18.

19.

20.

21.

Spotted Bunny

by Jimmy Kane
Age 10, Level II

This model was Inspired by Jon Montroll's Cow published in
<u>Origami Inside-out</u> and based heavily on Toshio Chino's "Rabbit" from
<u>The Magic of Origami</u> by Alice Grey and Kunnihiko Kasahara.

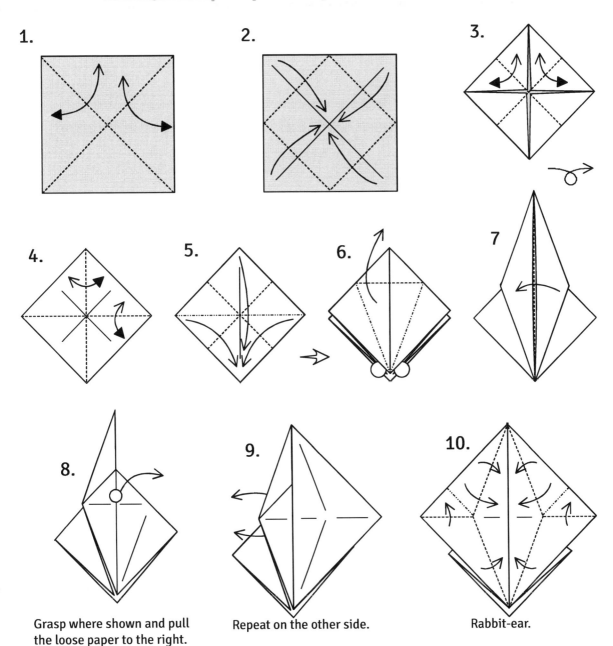

1.

2.

3.

4.

5.

6.

7

8.

Grasp where shown and pull
the loose paper to the right.

9.

Repeat on the other side.

10.

Rabbit-ear.

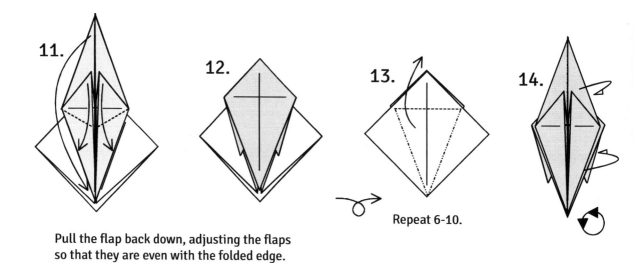

11.

Pull the flap back down, adjusting the flaps so that they are even with the folded edge.

12.

13.

Repeat 6-10.

14.

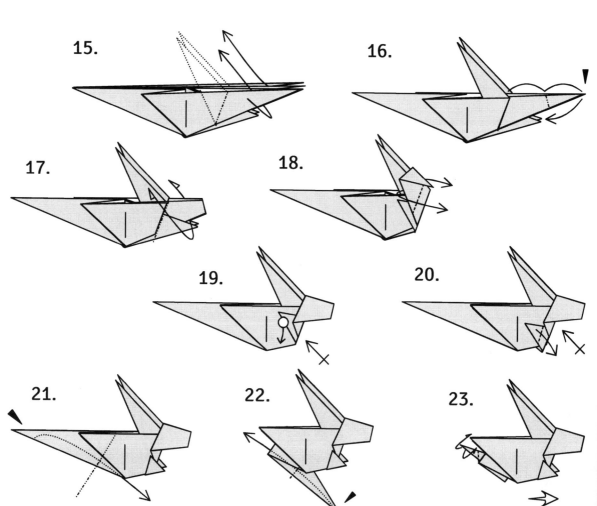

15.

16.

17.

18.

19.

20.

21.

22.

23.

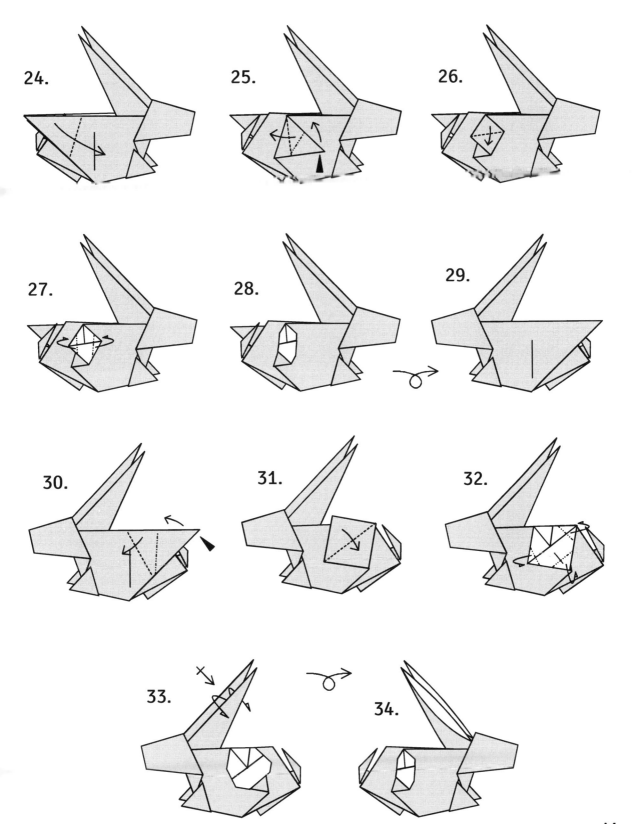

24.

25.

26.

27.

28.

29.

30.

31.

32.

33.

34.

Manatee

by Gabriel Willow
Age 14, Level II

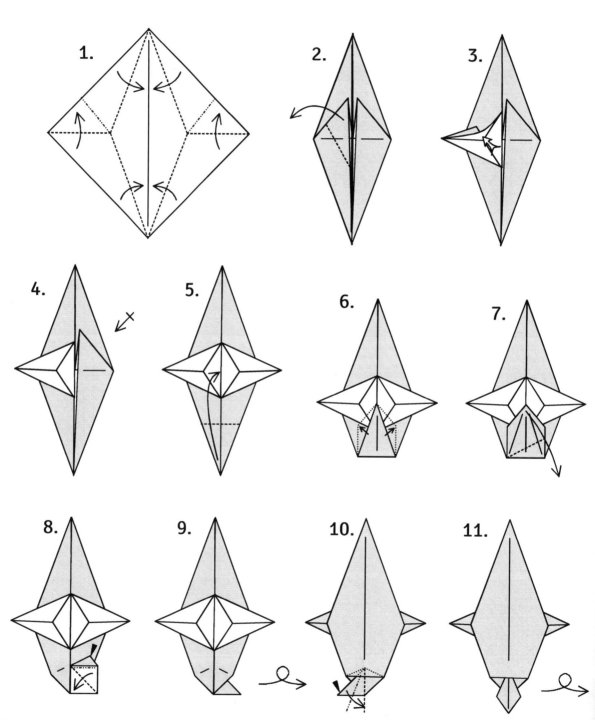

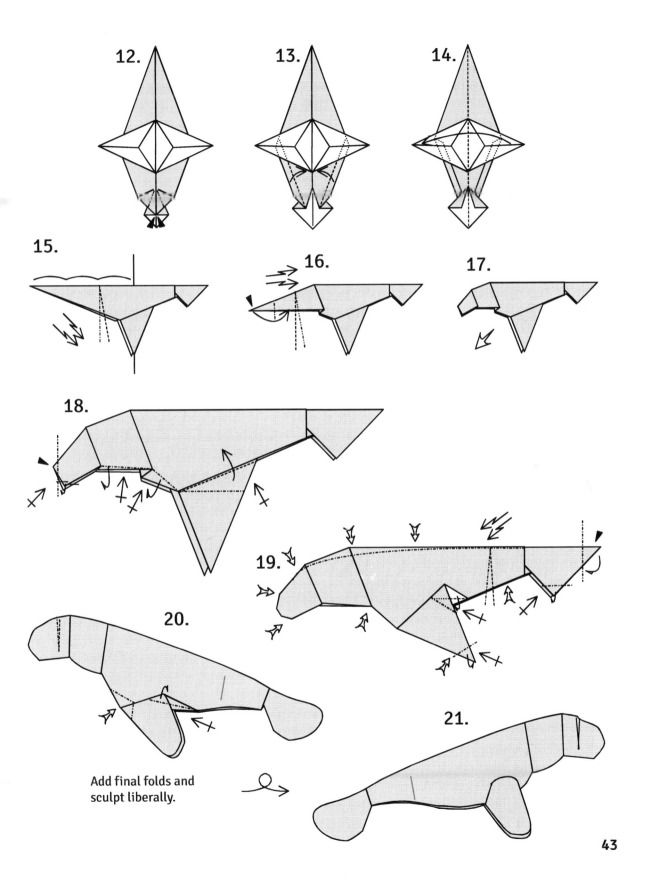

12.

13.

14.

15.

16.

17.

18.

19.

20.

Add final folds and
sculpt liberally.

21.

Perching Hawk

by Eric Anderson
Age 14, Level II

Based on John Montroll's "Ramphorinchus" from his book Prehistoric Origami.

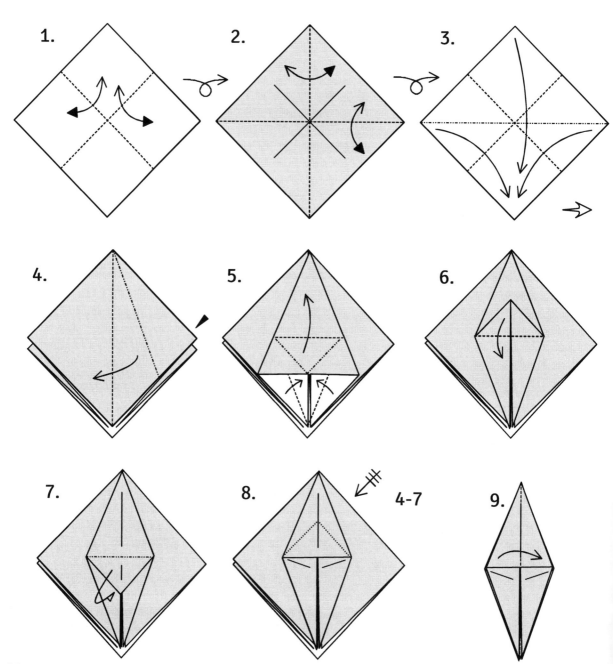

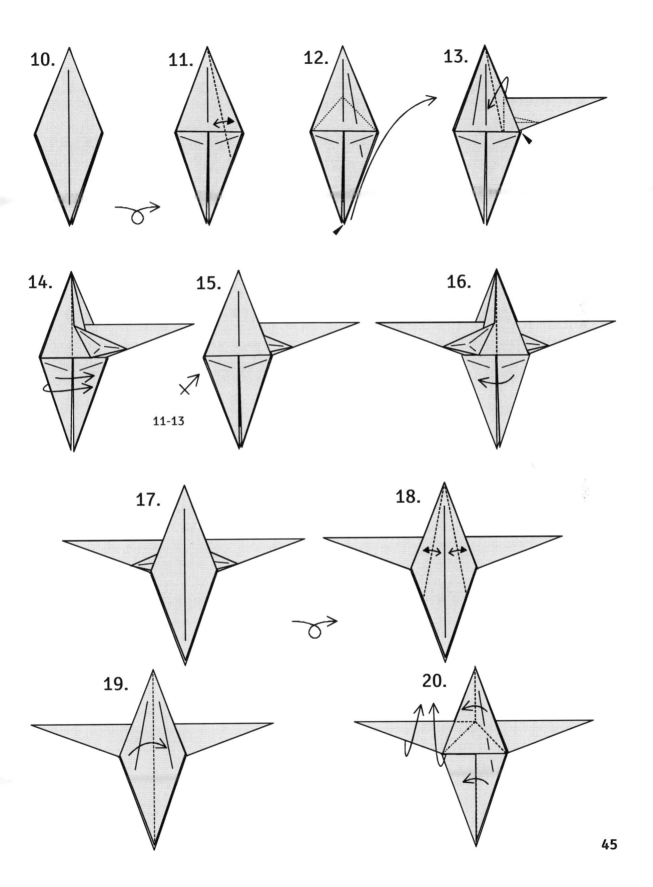

10.

11.

12.

13.

14.

15.

11-13

16.

17.

18.

19.

20.

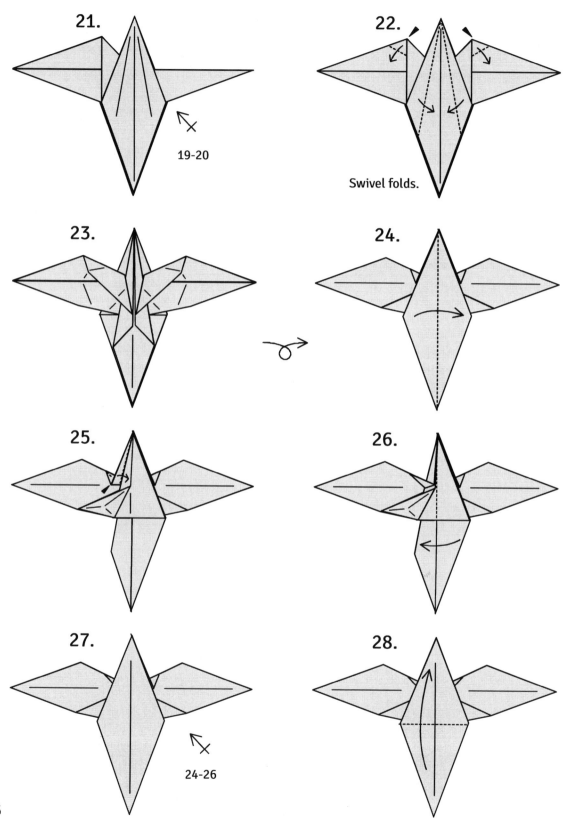

21.

19-20

22.

Swivel folds.

23.

24.

25.

24-26

26.

27.

28.

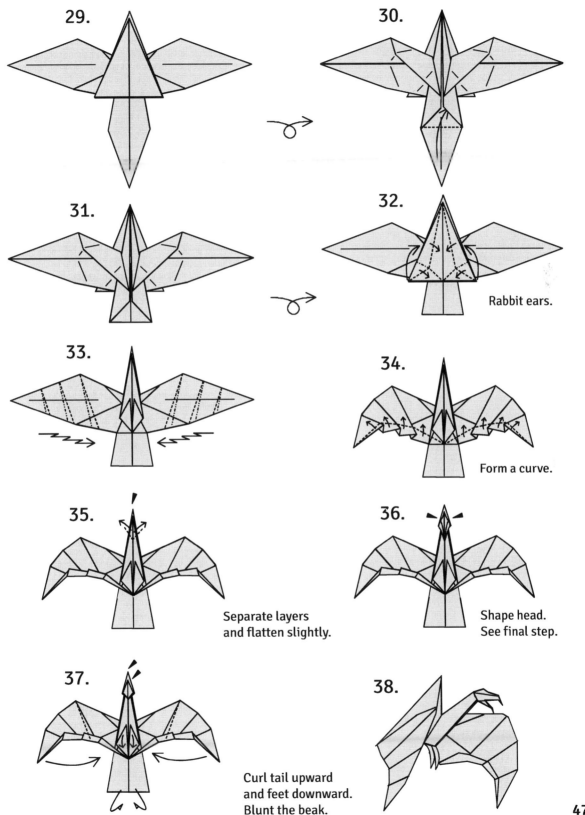

29.

30.

31.

32.

Rabbit ears.

33.

34.

Form a curve.

35.

Separate layers
and flatten slightly.

36.

Shape head.
See final step.

37.

Curl tail upward
and feet downward.
Blunt the beak.

38.

47

Penguin

by Michael LaFosse
Age 14, Level II

1.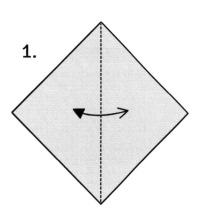

2.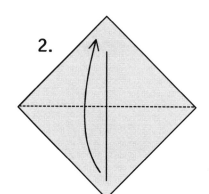

3.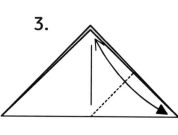

4.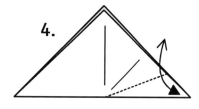

5.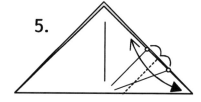

6.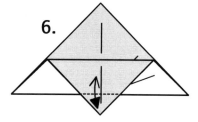

7.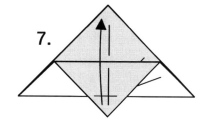

8.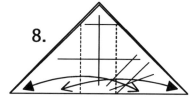

9.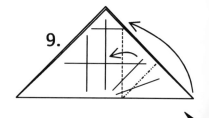

10.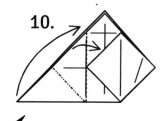

11.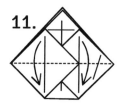

12.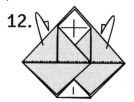

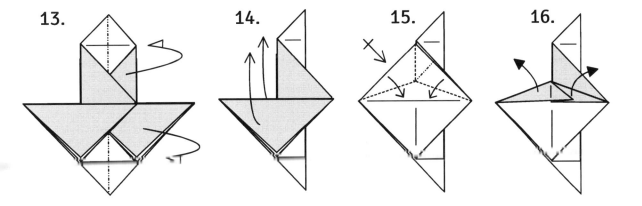

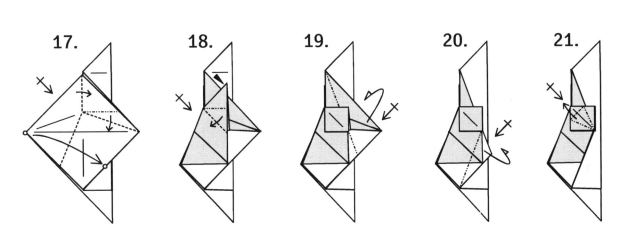

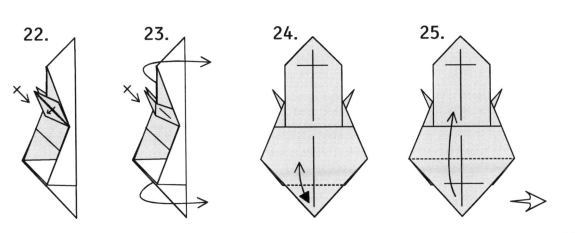

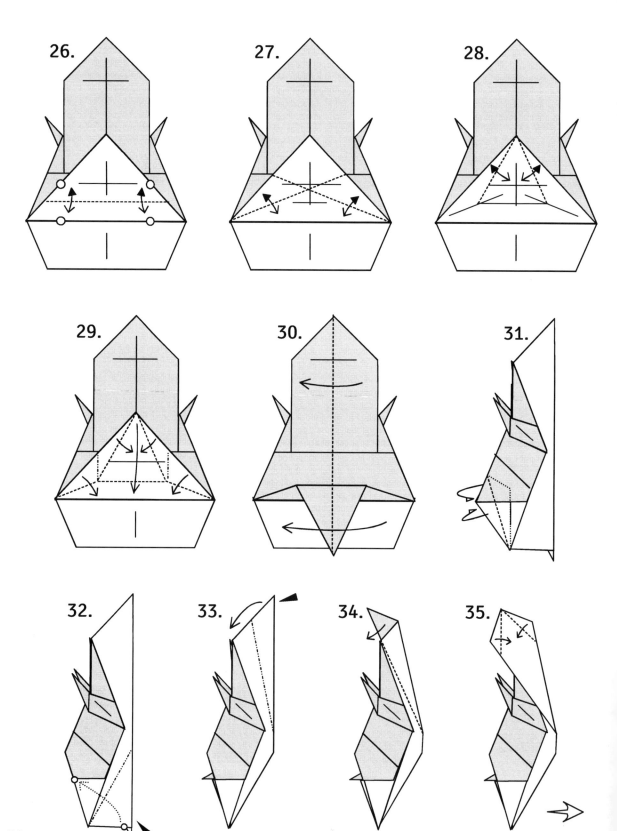

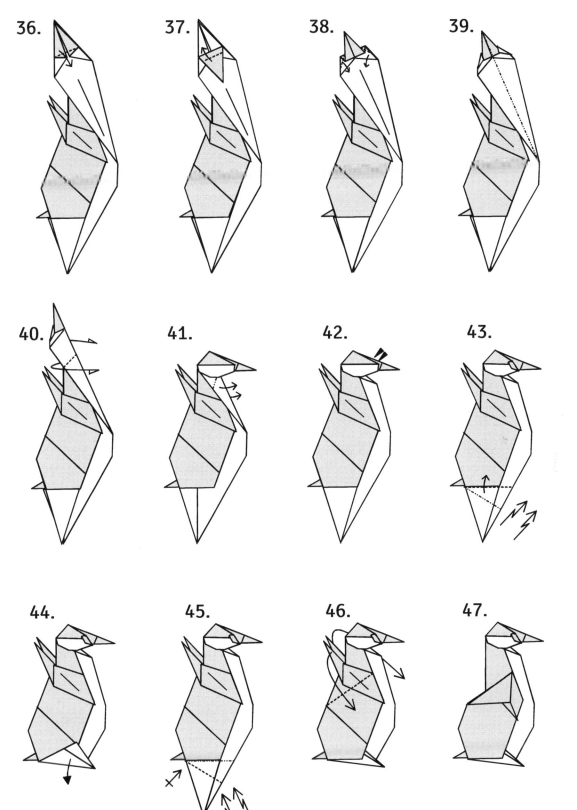

36.

37.

38.

39.

40.

41.

42.

43.

44.

45.

46.

47.

Tower Boxes

by Winson Chan
Age 17, Level II

Tower Boxes - Bottom Unit

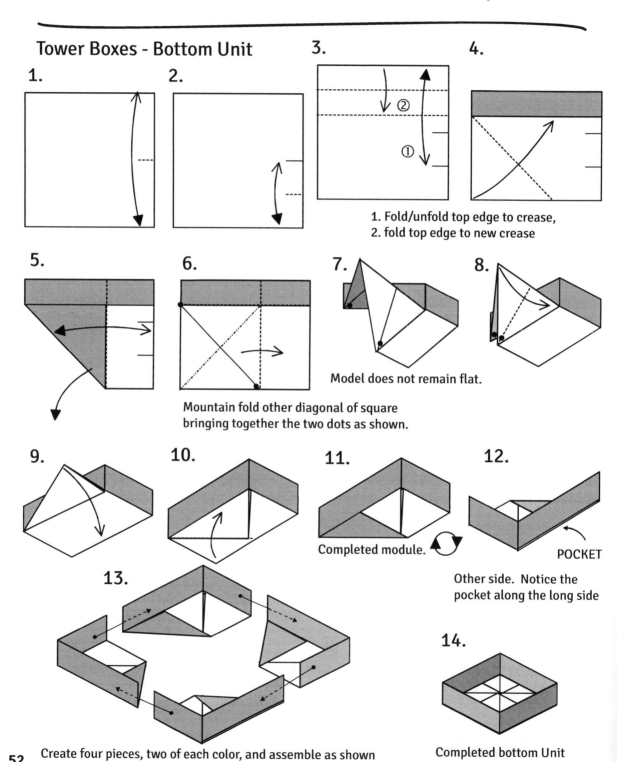

1.

2.

3.

4.

1. Fold/unfold top edge to crease,
2. fold top edge to new crease

5.

6.

7.

Model does not remain flat.

8.

Mountain fold other diagonal of square
bringing together the two dots as shown.

9.

10.

11.

Completed module.

12.

POCKET

Other side. Notice the
pocket along the long side

13.

Create four pieces, two of each color, and assemble as shown

14.

Completed bottom Unit

52

Tower Boxes - Top Unit

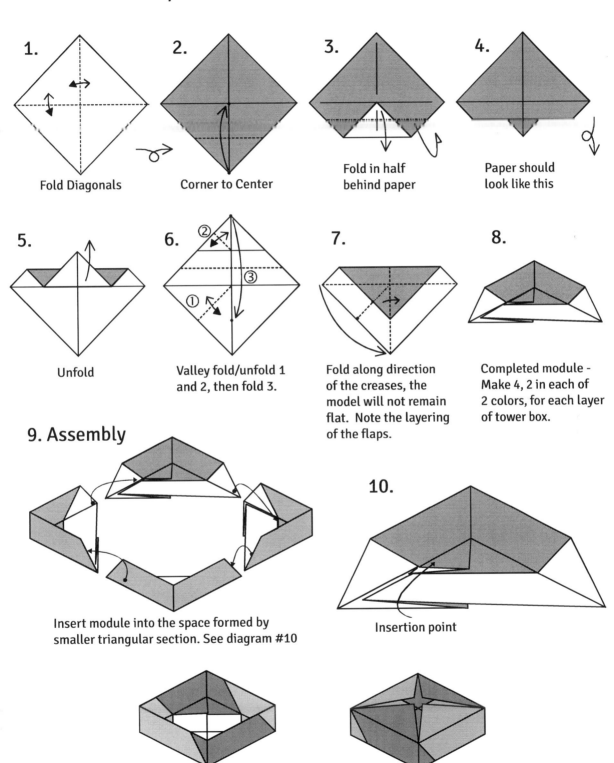

1. Fold Diagonals

2. Corner to Center

3. Fold in half behind paper

4. Paper should look like this

5. Unfold

6. Valley fold/unfold 1 and 2, then fold 3.

7. Fold along direction of the creases, the model will not remain flat. Note the layering of the flaps.

8. Completed module - Make 4, 2 in each of 2 colors, for each layer of tower box.

9. Assembly

Insert module into the space formed by smaller triangular section. See diagram #10

10. Insertion point

VIEW FROM THE BOTTOM

VIEW FROM THE TOP

53

Assembly of Middle Section

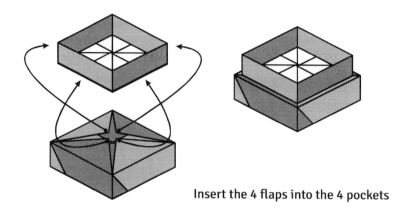

Insert the 4 flaps into the 4 pockets

Assembly of Base

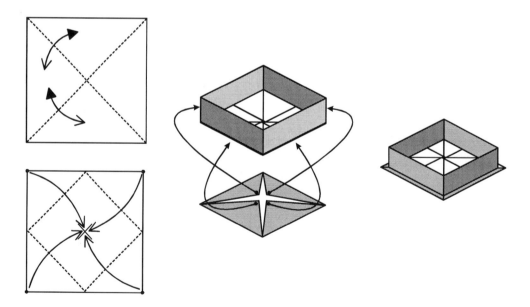

The base of the tower box is identical to the bottom section, but with the addition of a fifth piece. Fold the 4 corners of the fifth sheet to the center, and insert into the pockets of bottom unit to form the base unit.

Tower Boxes - Assembly of Cover

The cover for the tower box is essentially the same as the top unit.
Step 1 to 5 are the same, start with the following step.

6.

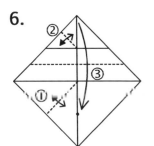

Fold/unfold 1 and 2. Fold 3 along line indicated. Notice fold 2 is now a mountain fold.

7.

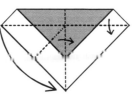

Fold along direction of the creases. Both layer of folded together model will not remain flat.

8.

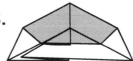

Completed module. Smaller triangular section is now underneath. Make 4 for cover of tower box.

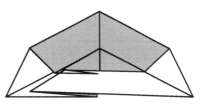

ENLARGED VIEW

Final Assembly

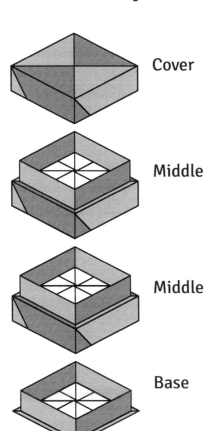

Cover

Middle

Middle

Base

9. Assembly

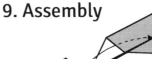

Insert module into the space formed by smaller triangular section.

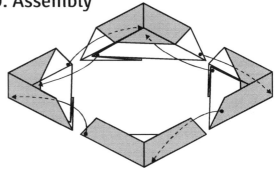

VIEW FROM THE BOTTOM

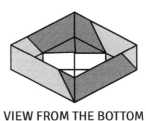

VIEW FROM THE TOP

Screaming Michael

by Daniel Stillman
Age 14, Level II

This model was inspired by and dedicated to Daniel's mentor
and teacher, Michael Shall, President emeritis of Origami U.S.A.

1.

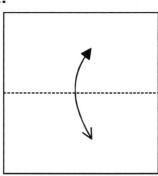

2.

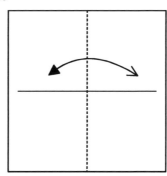

3.

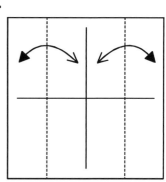

4.

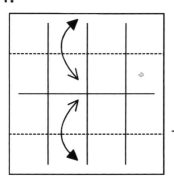

5.

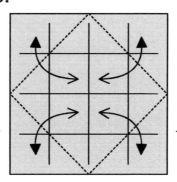

6.

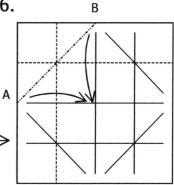

Following the creases, bring
points A and B to the center.

7.

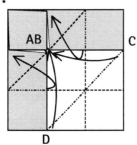

Do the same with C & D.

8.

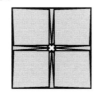

Windmill base.

9.

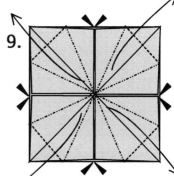

10.

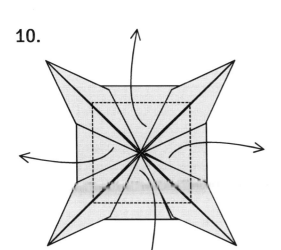

11.

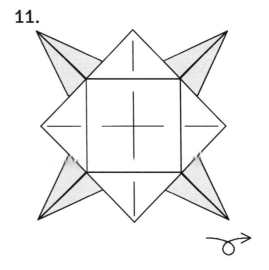

12.

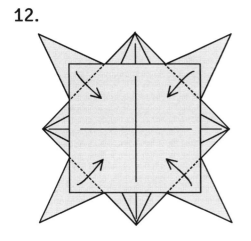

13.

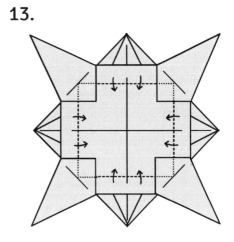

14.

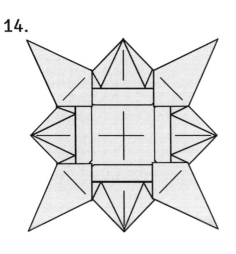

15.

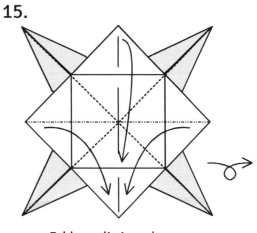

Fold a preliminary base
on the white area

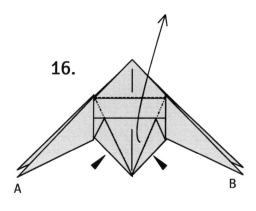

16.

Fold a petal fold on the flap (as referenced in the preliminary base in the previous step. The points A & B will spread open and remain on thier respective sides.

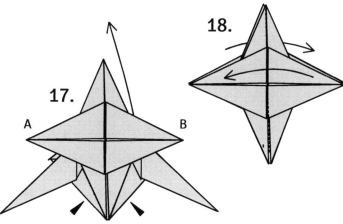

17.

18.

Repeat the petal fold on the other side.

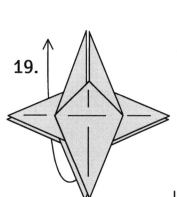

19.

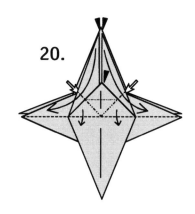

20.

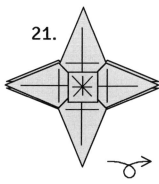

21.

Insert fingers where shown and squash fold the two points, spread squashing the inner triangle.

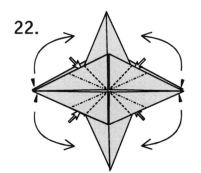

22.

Squash fold the four petals inserting fingers where shown being careful to distribute inside flaps evenly!

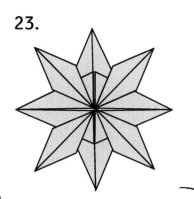

23.

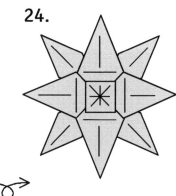

24.

Surfer on a Wave

by Jeremy Shafer
Age 14, Level 11+

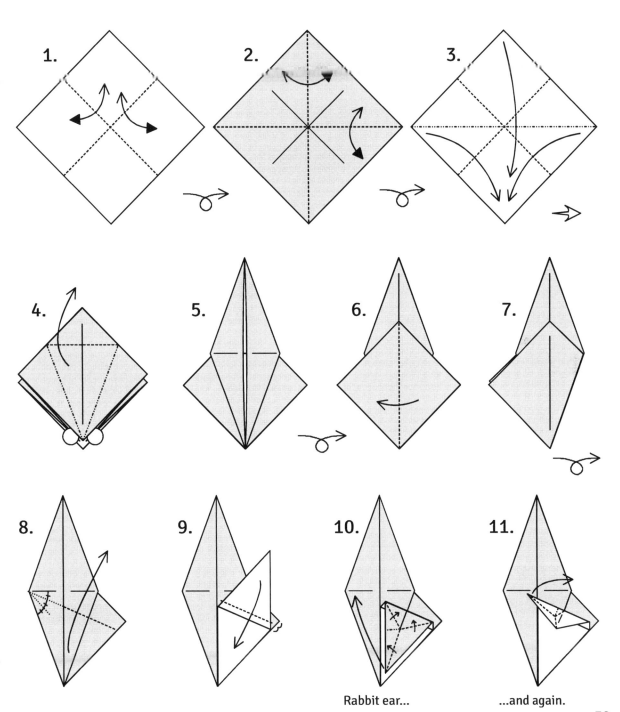

1.

2.

3.

4.

5.

6.

7.

8.

9.

10.

Rabbit ear...

11.

...and again.

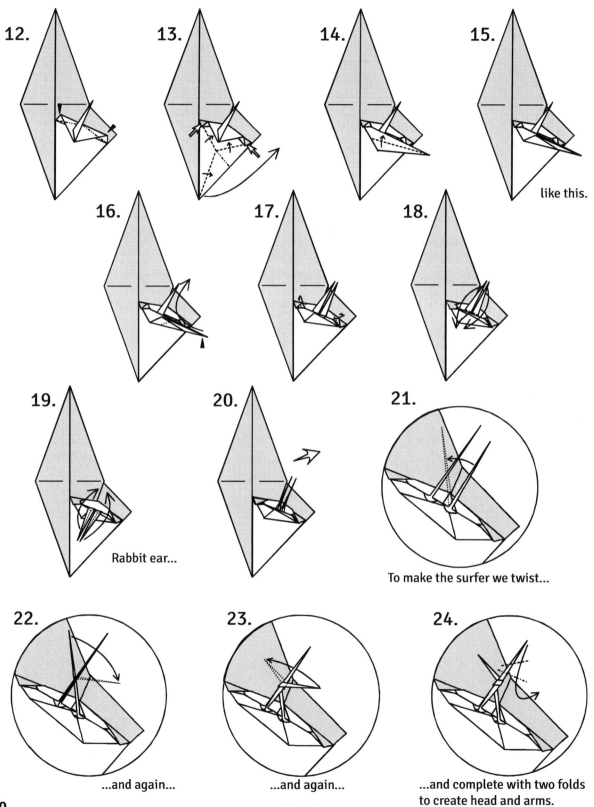

12.

13.

14.

15. like this.

16.

17.

18.

19. Rabbit ear...

20.

21. To make the surfer we twist...

22. ...and again...

23. ...and again...

24. ...and complete with two folds to create head and arms.

25. **26.** **27.**

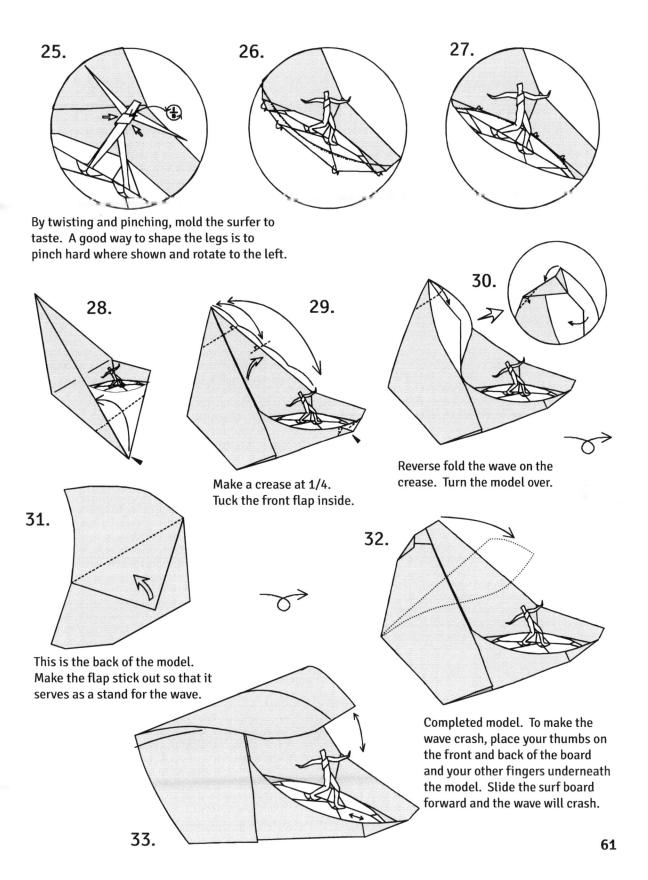

By twisting and pinching, mold the surfer to taste. A good way to shape the legs is to pinch hard where shown and rotate to the left.

28. **29.** **30.**

Make a crease at 1/4. Tuck the front flap inside.

Reverse fold the wave on the crease. Turn the model over.

31.

This is the back of the model. Make the flap stick out so that it serves as a stand for the wave.

32.

Completed model. To make the wave crash, place your thumbs on the front and back of the board and your other fingers underneath the model. Slide the surf board forward and the wave will crash.

33.

Balloon Man

by Alasdair Post-Quinn
Age 17, Level II+

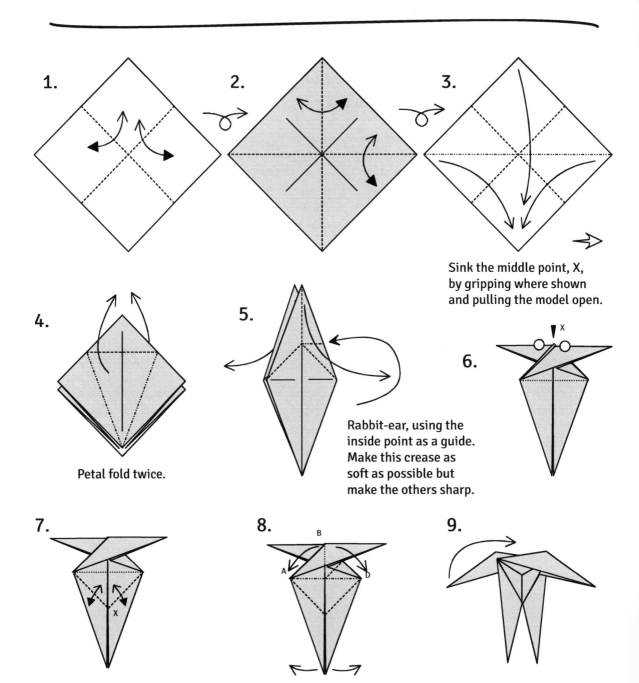

1.

2.

3.

Sink the middle point, X, by gripping where shown and pulling the model open.

4.

5.

6.

Petal fold twice.

Rabbit-ear, using the inside point as a guide. Make this crease as soft as possible but make the others sharp.

7.

8.

9.

Note new location of point X. Pre-crease using it as a guide.

Bring Point A to B and point C to D using the existing creases pinching the inside flap closed. The model will become 3D!

Adjust rear flap so that it is in the middle.

10.

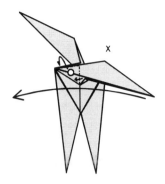

Grasp the flap indicated by the white circle and pull it over. This will cause point X to jump from the right to the left and settle in the same place on the opposite side. Be careful not to trap the rear flap.

11.

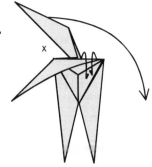

Do the same on the other side, pulling the flap to the front.

12.

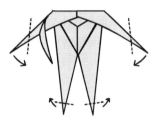

Valley fold (to taste) to make hands and feet.

13.

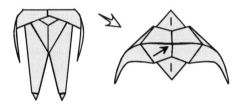

Note the hole located on the top. Separate the flaps and and the stem of an inflated helium balloon may be placed inside. Also, ballast (coins, sand, etc.) can also be added to weightdown the model. If the right amount of ballast is added, "Ballon Man" can be made to float in mid air or walk across the floor at the whim of local breezes.

Flapping Bat

by Julia Einbond
Age 12, Level II

1.

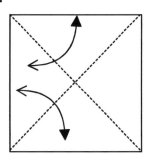

2.

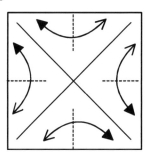

3.

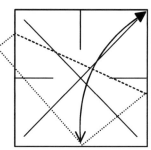

Bring the corner to the edge and unfold.

4.

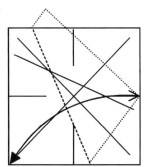

Repeat on the opposite corner.

5.

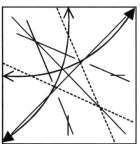

Repeat on the remaining two.

6.

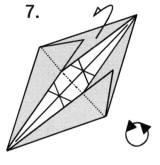

7.

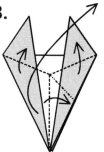

8.

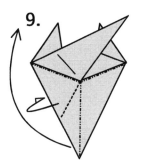

9.

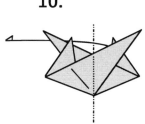

This is the same as step 8.

10.

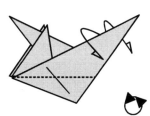

11.

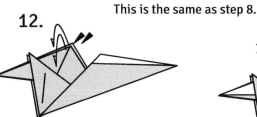

12.

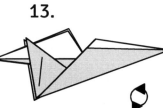

Wrap the hidden white layers around the colored layers.

13.

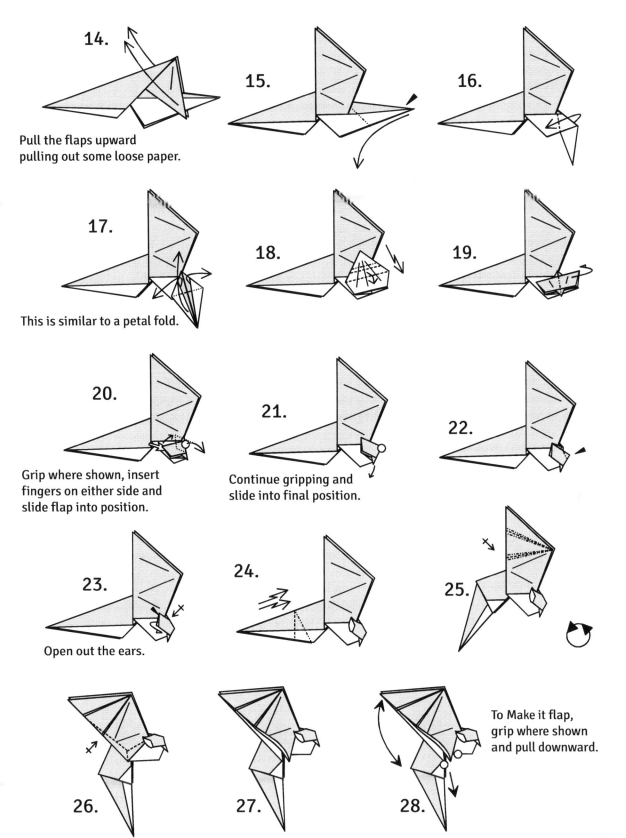

14. Pull the flaps upward pulling out some loose paper.

15.

16.

17. This is similar to a petal fold.

18.

19.

20. Grip where shown, insert fingers on either side and slide flap into position.

21. Continue gripping and slide into final position.

22.

23. Open out the ears.

24.

25.

26.

27.

28. To Make it flap, grip where shown and pull downward.

Weasel

by Gabriel Willow
Age 11, Level 11+

1.

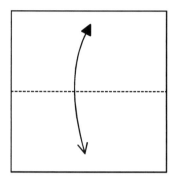

2.

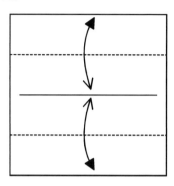

3.

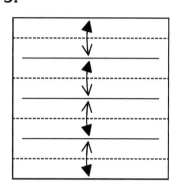

4.

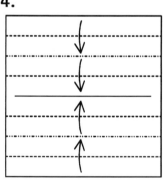

5.

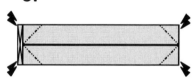

6.

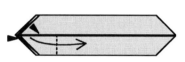

7.

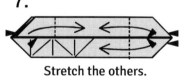

Stretch the others.

8. Stretch the point.

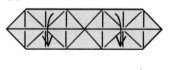

9.

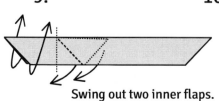

Swing out two inner flaps.

10.

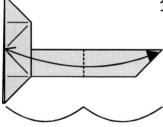

11.

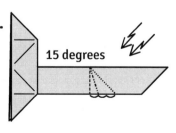

15 degrees

12.

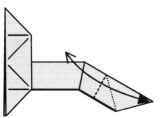

Fold and unfold using the internal structures as a guideline.

13.

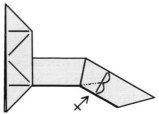

Carefully pinch the mountain fold into place in front and behind.

14.

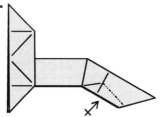

Again, carefully pinch the next mountain fold into place in front and behind.

15.

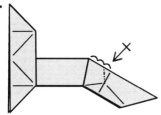

Pinch the final mountain fold into place in front and behind.

16.

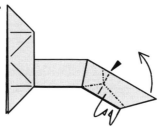

Put the construction in place by pushing in where shown while swinging the point upward and the lower flaps inward.

17.

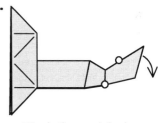

Pinch the model where shown and rotate the tail downward.

18.

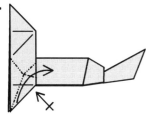

19.

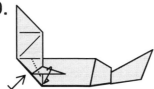

20.

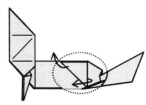

Cut away view. Pull out the trapped layers.

21.

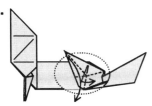

22.

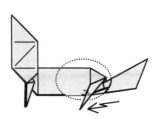

23.

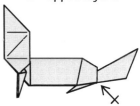

24.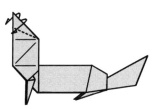

25.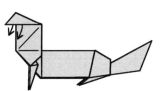

Pull down the hidden layers.

26.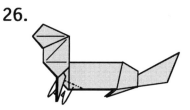

27.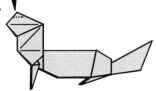

28.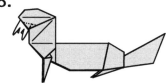

29.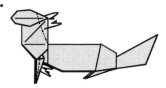

30.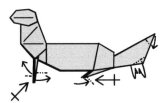

31.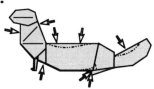

32

White Ibis

by Gabriel Willow
Age 14, Level 11+

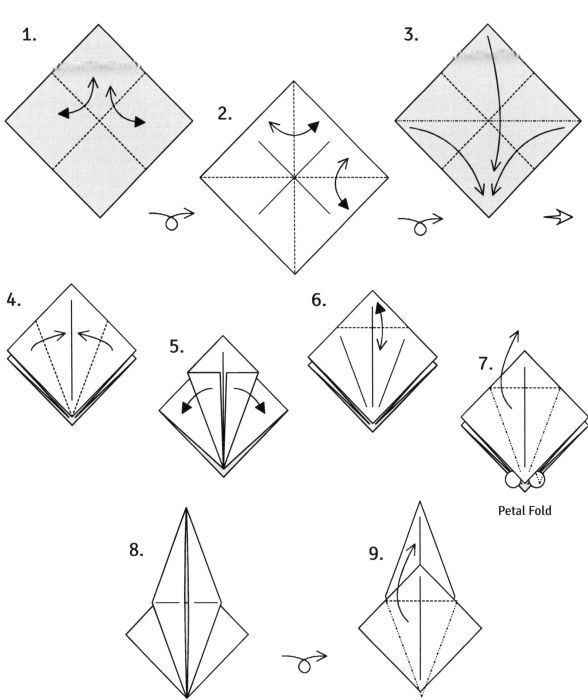

1.

2.

3.

4.

5.

6.

7.

Petal Fold

8.

9.

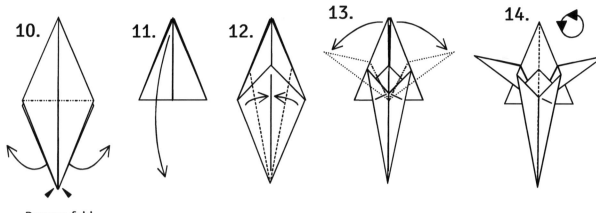

10.

Reverse fold.

11.

12.

13.

14.

15.

16.

17.

Carefully slide the paper
back as far as it will go
on both sides of both legs.

18.

19.

20.

21.

22.

23.

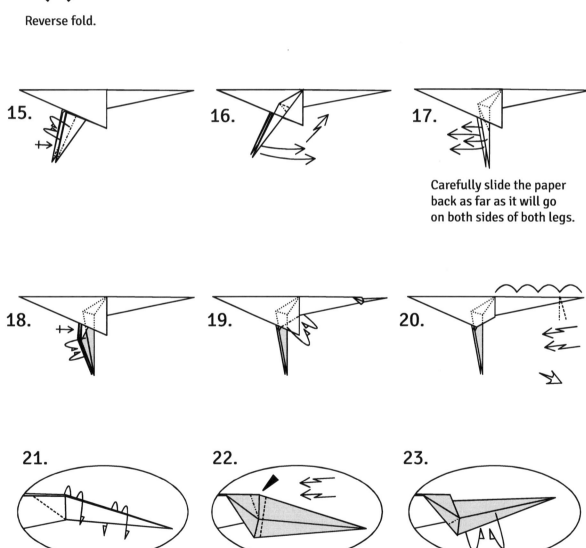

24.

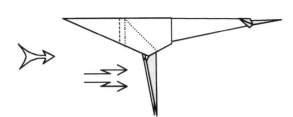

25.

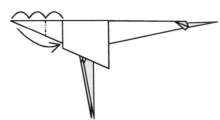

26.

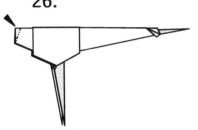

27.

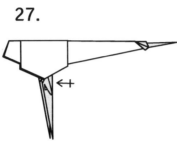

28.

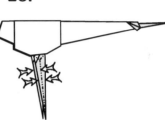

29.

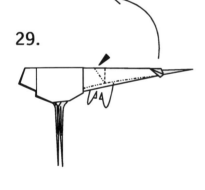

30.

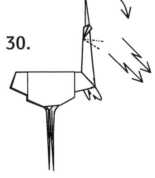

31.

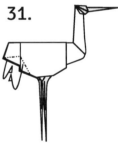

32.

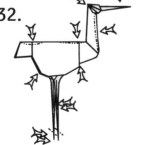

33.

Heron

by Gabriel Willow
Age 15, Level II+

1.

2.

3.

4.

5.

6.

7.

Petal Fold

8.

9.

10.

11.

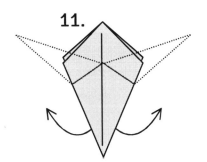

12.

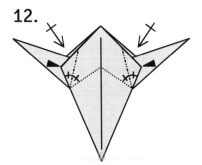

Sink triangularly using the
hidden landmarks. This will
leave two small flaps sticking out.

13.

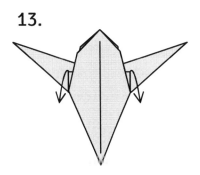

14.

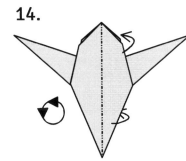

15.

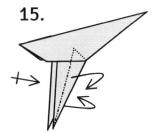

16.

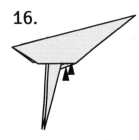

17.

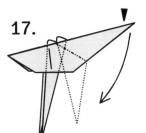

18.

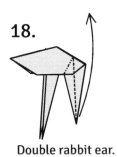

Double rabbit ear.

19.

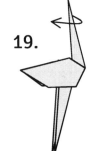

20.

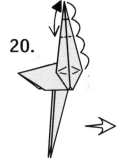

21.

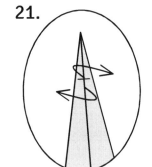

Close-up view. Carefully
open the two layers on
each side.

22.

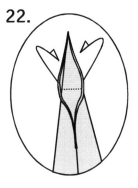

Wrap only the outer layer
behind on the 1/4th mark
made previously.

23.

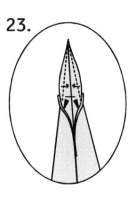

Fold the inner layers
back in. Flatten out
the outer layers.

24.

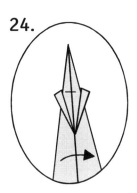

25.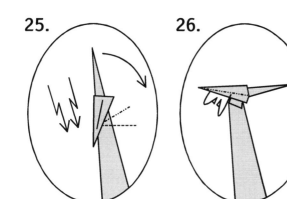

26.

27.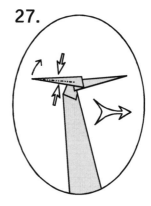

28.

29.

30.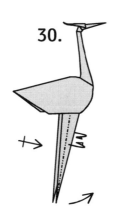

31.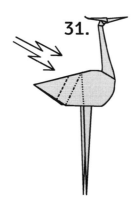

32.

33.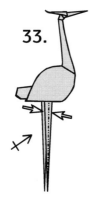

34.

35.

Opossum

by Aaron Einbond
Age 15, Level II+

1.

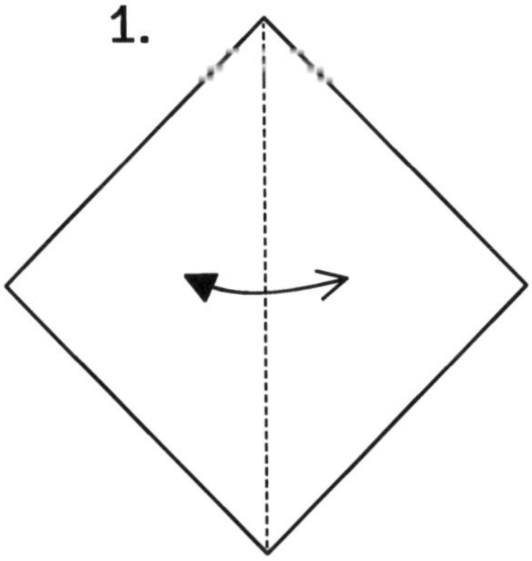

2.

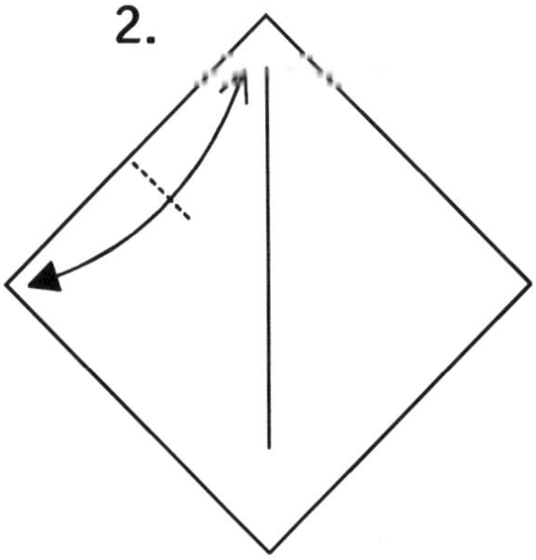

3.

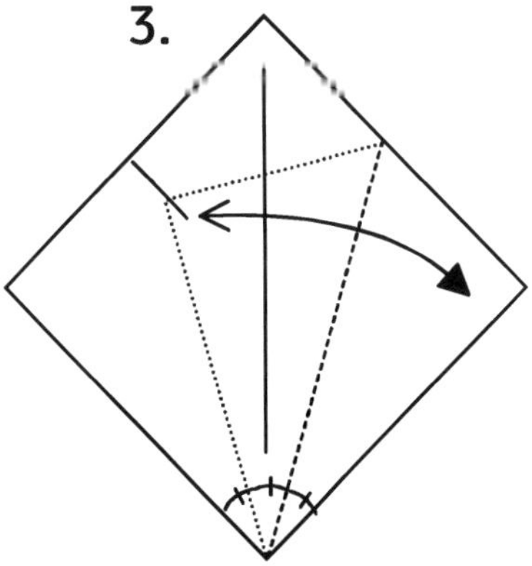

4.

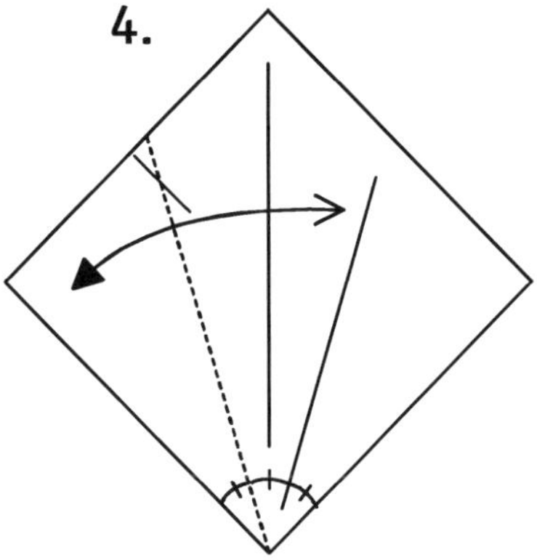

5.

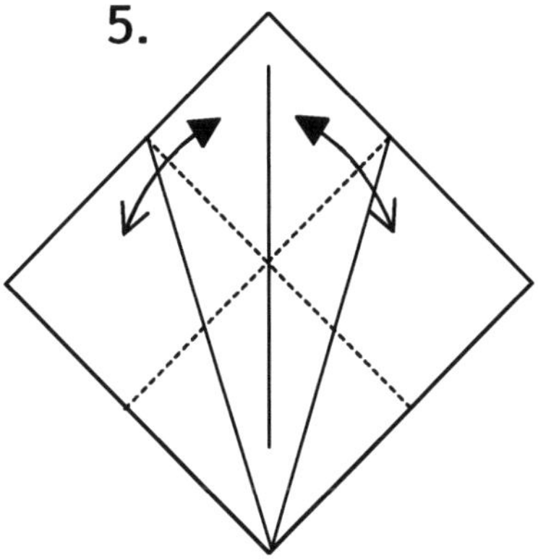

6.

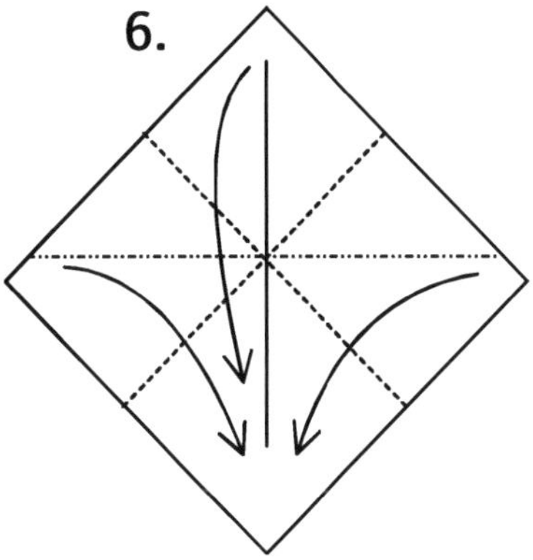

7.

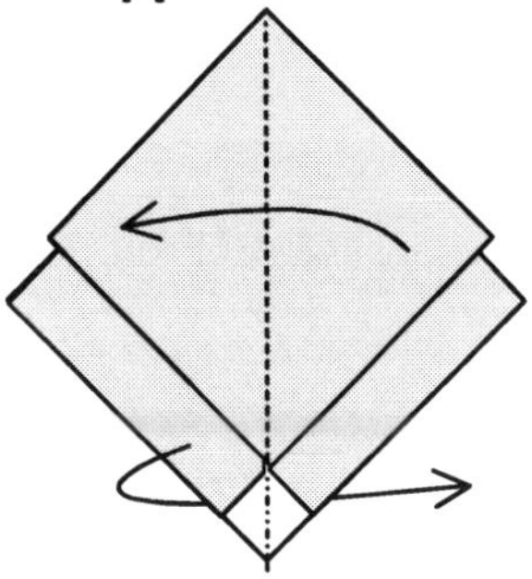

8.

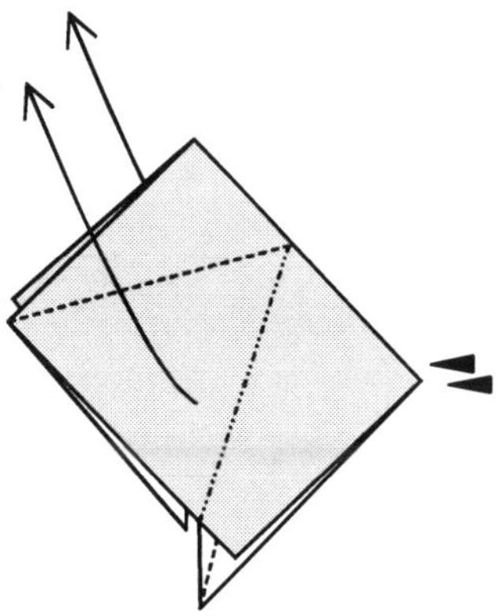

9.

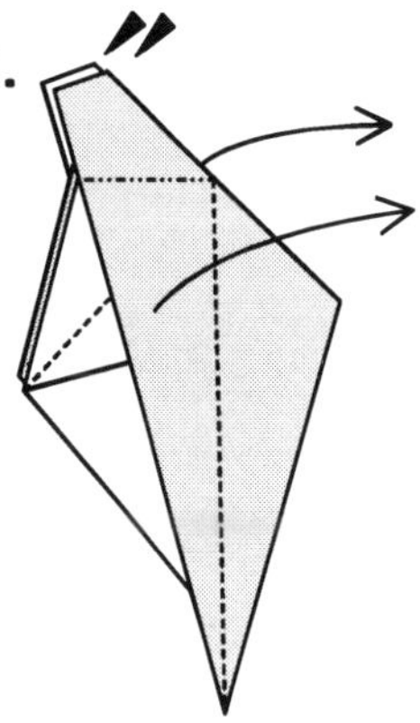

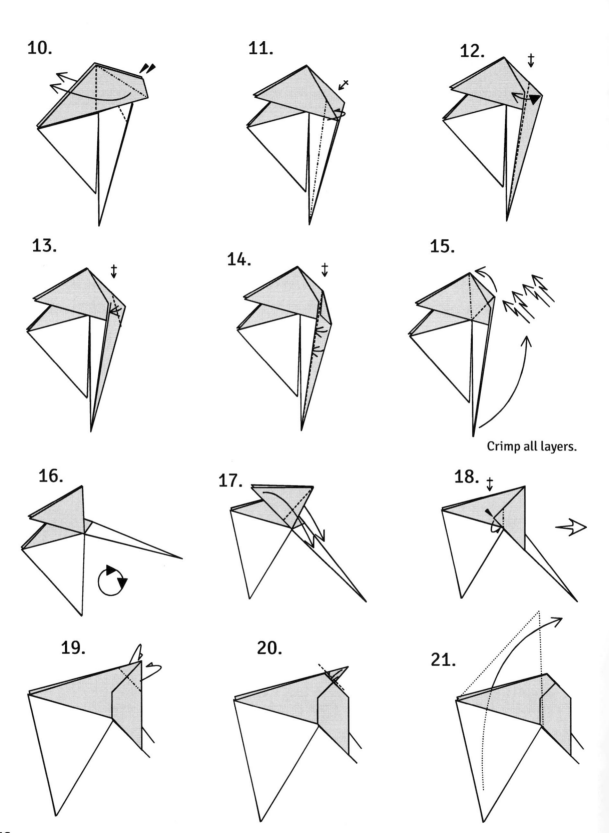

10.

11.

12.

13.

14.

15.

Crimp all layers.

16.

17.

18.

19.

20.

21.

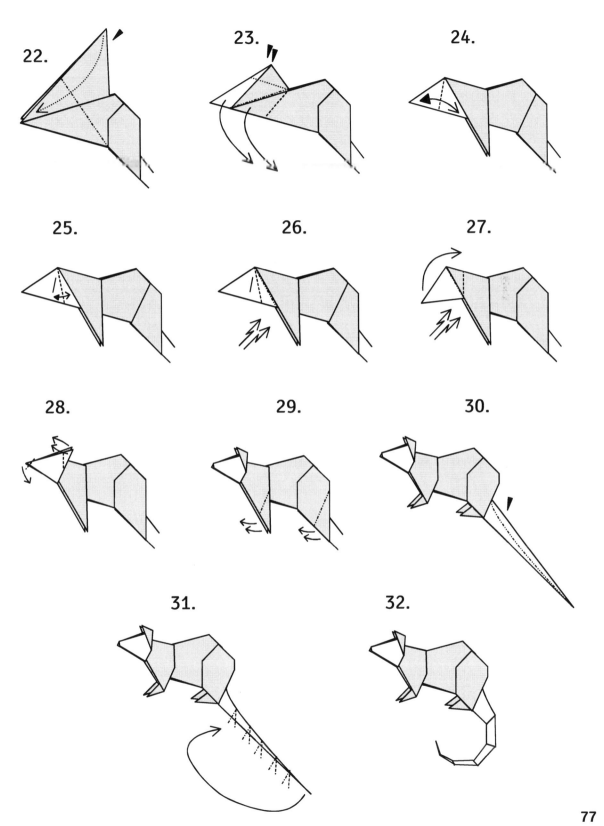

22.

23.

24.

25.

26.

27.

28.

29.

30.

31.

32.

Pot-bellied Pig

by Paul Fischer
Age 16, Level 11+

1.

2.

3.

4.

5.

6.

7.

8.

9.

10.

11.

12.

13.

14.

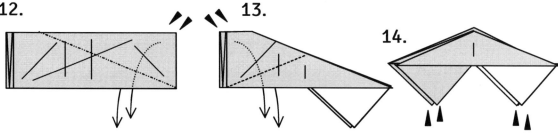

15.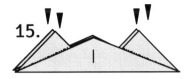

16.

17.

18. Pull out some loose paper.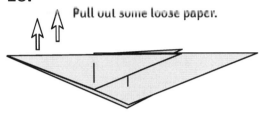

19.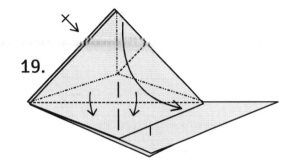

20.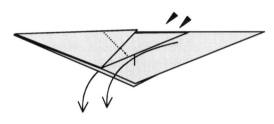

21.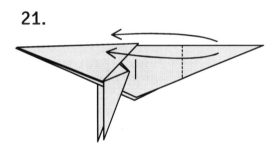

22.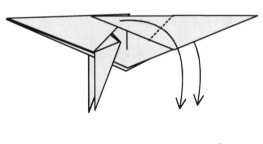

23.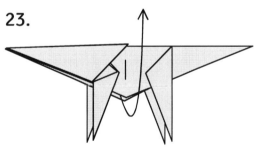

24.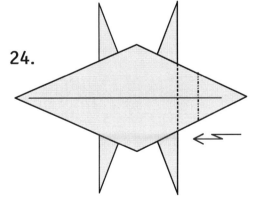

25.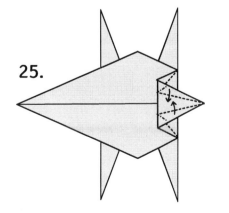

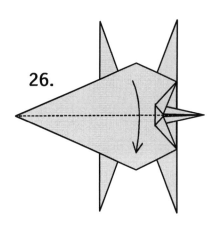

26.

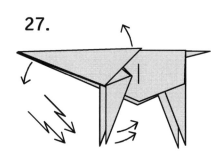

27.

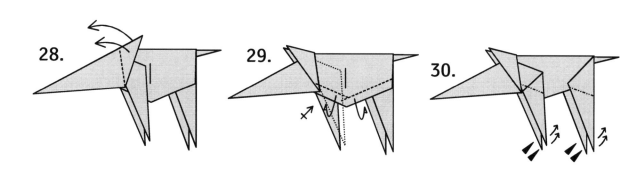

28.

29.

30.

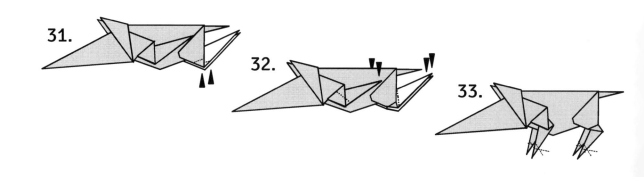

31.

32.

33.

34.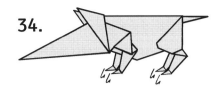

35.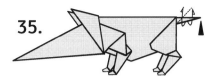

37.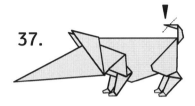

36.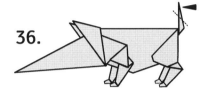

38.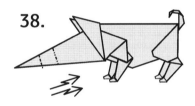

39.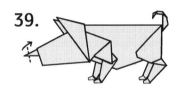

40.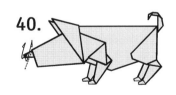

41.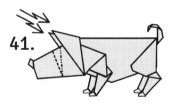

Beaver

by Gabriel Willow
Age 16, Level III

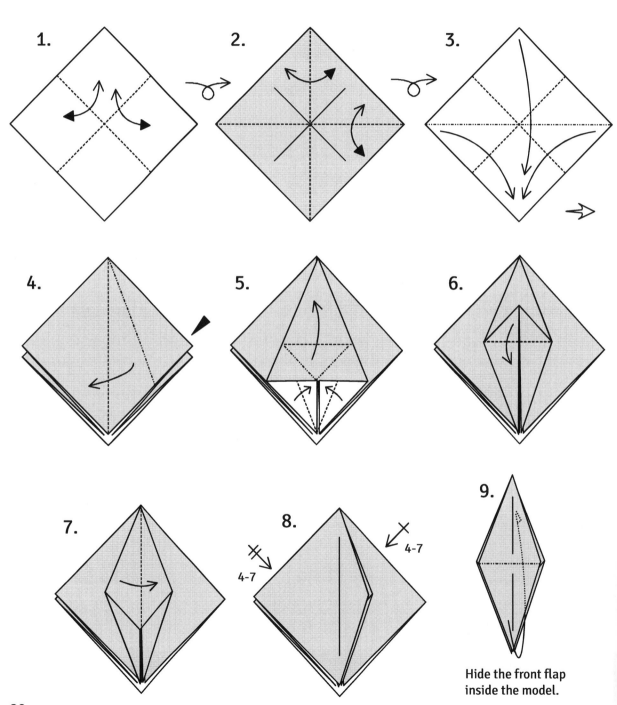

9. Hide the front flap inside the model.

10.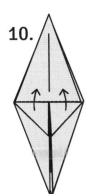

11.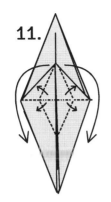

12.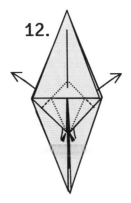

Reverse fold as far as possible, using the internal structures as a guideline.

13.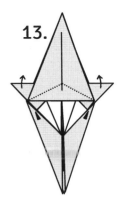

Again, reverse fold as far as possible, sliding the colored paper upward.

14.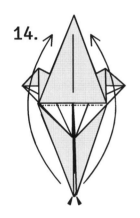

15.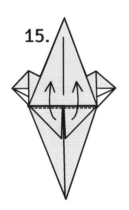

16.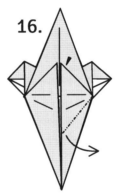

17.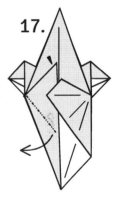

18.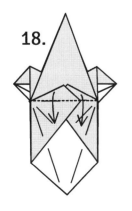

19.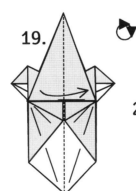

Pull a single layer upward on either side, as you do this a crimp will naturally form inside, and the back will move downward.

20.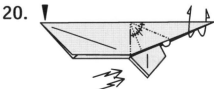

21.

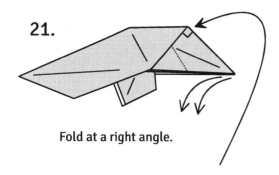

Fold at a right angle.

22.

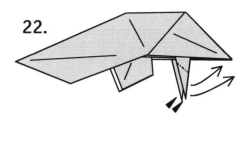

23.

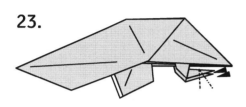

24.

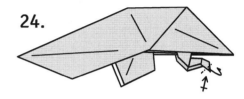

25.

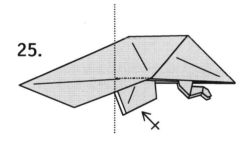

26.

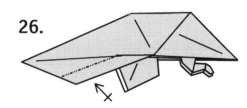

27.

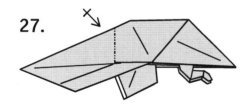

28.

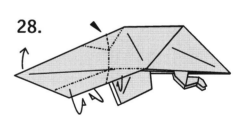

29.

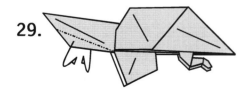

30.

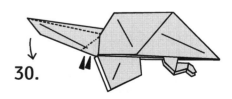

Flatten out the tail, forming a
small ridge down the center.

31.

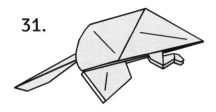

32.

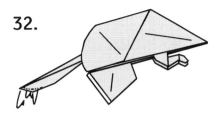

33.

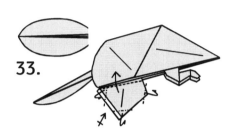

34.

35.

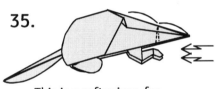

This is a soft crimp, for sculpting purposes only.

36.

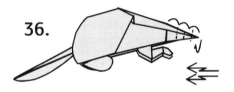

37.

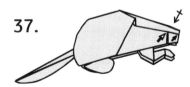

Using a pencil, form eyes & nostrils.

38.

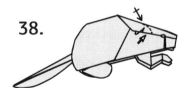

39.

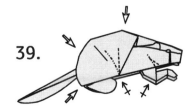

40.

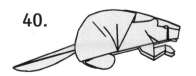

Folding the Preliminary Base

by Jeremy Shafer
Age 16, Level III

1.

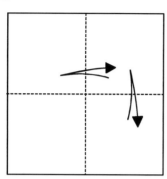

2.

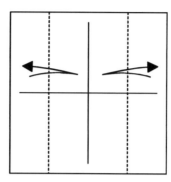

3.

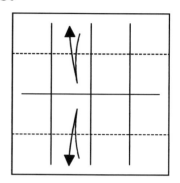

4.

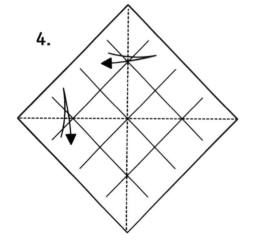

5.

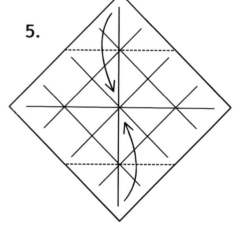

6.

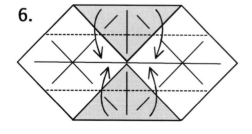

7.

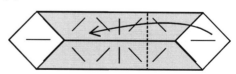

8.

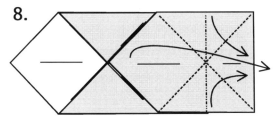

Fold a waterbomb base.

9.

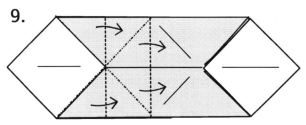

And fold another...

10.

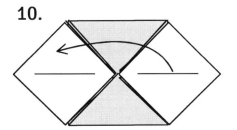

Repeat steps 10-35 from
"Folding the Blintz Base."

11.

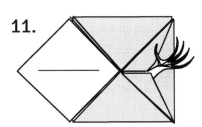

Like this.

12.

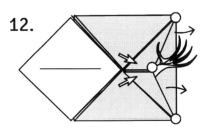

Slide the hand as far to
the right as possible.

13.

10-12

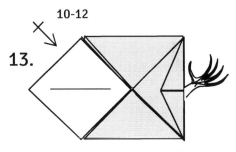

Repeat steps 10-12 on the other
side, reverseing the folds so that
a left hand is created.

14.

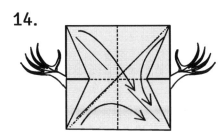

Fold a preliminary base.

15.

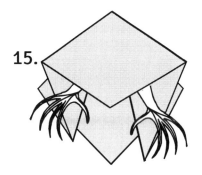

87

Folding the Blintz Base

by Jeremy Shafer
Age 16, Level III

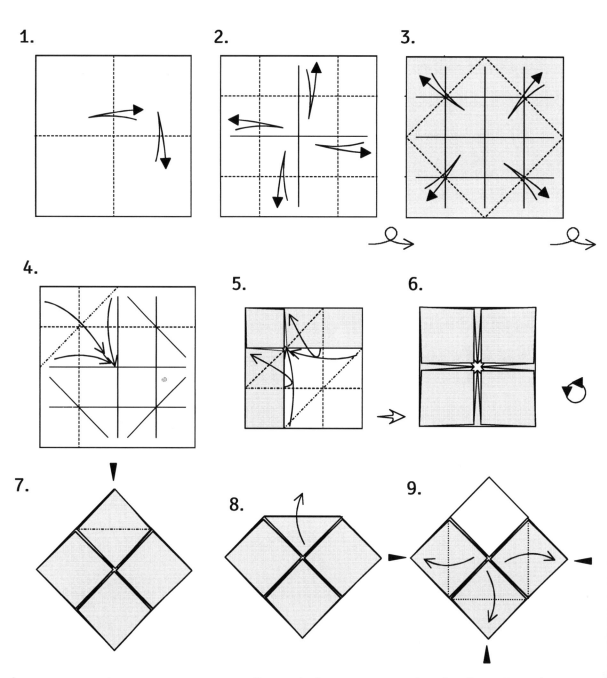

1.

2.

3.

4.

5.

6.

7.

8.

9.

Repeat the last two steps on the other flaps. Note, this can be done in one step to aviod making a crease.

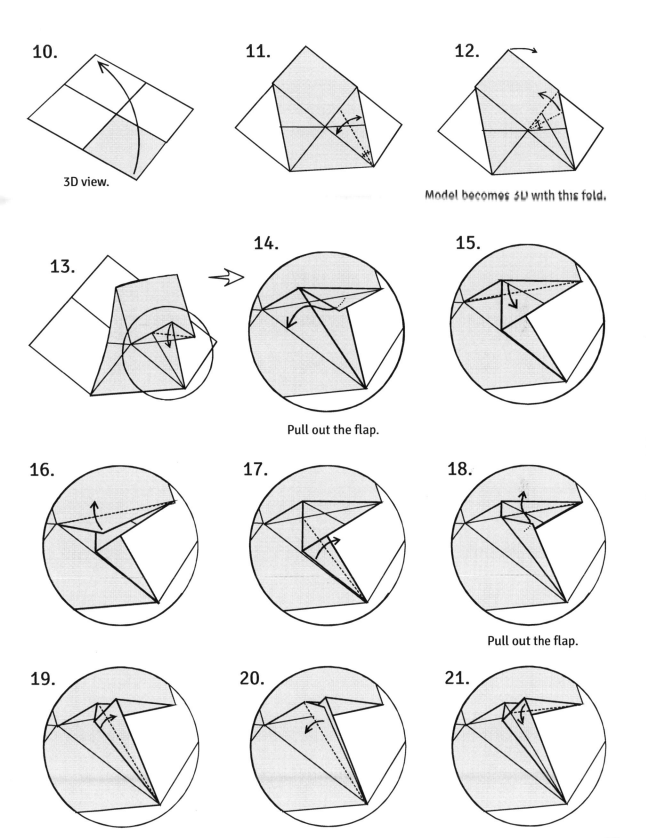

10.

3D view.

11.

12.

Model becomes 3D with this fold.

13.

14.

Pull out the flap.

15.

16.

17.

18.

Pull out the flap.

19.

20.

21.

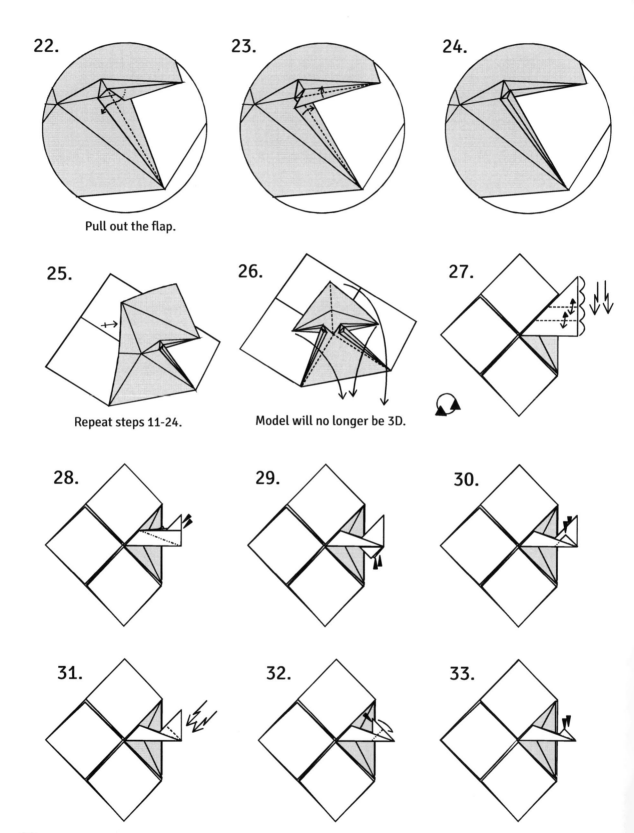

22.

Pull out the flap.

23.

24.

25.

Repeat steps 11-24.

26.

Model will no longer be 3D.

27.

28.

29.

30.

31.

32.

33.

34.

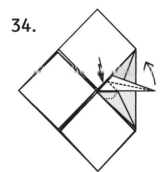

Crimp the wrist, swinging the hand upward, to do this you will need to closed-sink the base of the wrist. Its final position is indicated by the dotted line.

35.

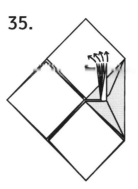

Spread the points and move the hand into position.

36.

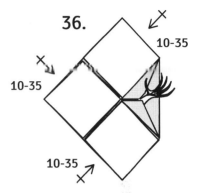

10-35

10-35

10-35

Repeat steps 10-35 on the other three corners.

37.

Curl the corners so that the hands are folding the paper.

38.

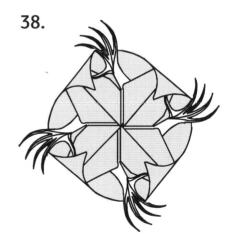

Rearing Dragon

by Marc Kirschenbaum
Age 16, Level II+

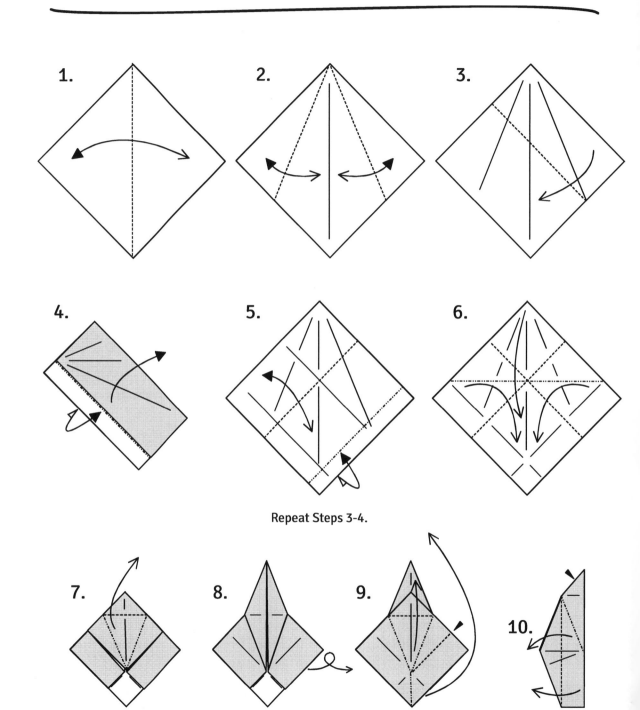

Repeat Steps 3-4.

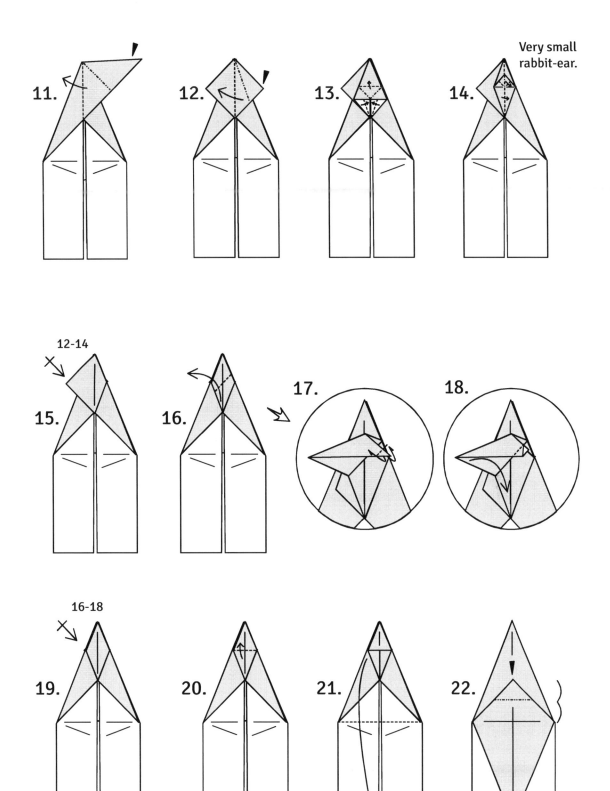

11.

12.

13.

14. Very small rabbit-ear.

15. 12-14

16.

17.

18.

19. 16-18

20.

21.

22.

93

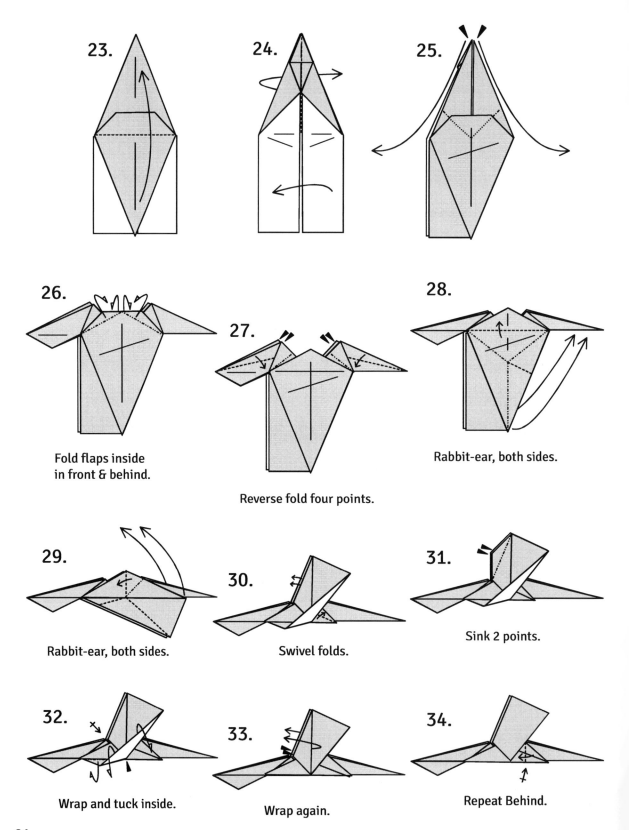

23.

24.

25.

26.

Fold flaps inside
in front & behind.

27.

Reverse fold four points.

28.

Rabbit-ear, both sides.

29.

Rabbit-ear, both sides.

30.

Swivel folds.

31.

Sink 2 points.

32.

Wrap and tuck inside.

33.

Wrap again.

34.

Repeat Behind.

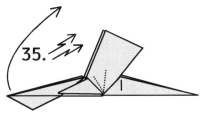 35.

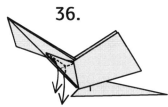 36.

Rabbit-ear, both sides.

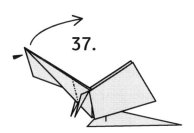 37.

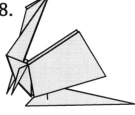 38.

Like this.

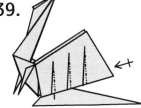 39.

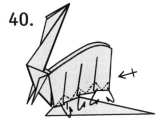 40.

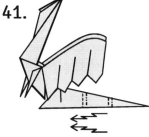 41.

 42.

43.

44.

45.

46.

47.

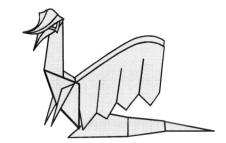

This is a view of the bottom of the head. Fold edges in softly to thin the jaw and expose the eyes.

Sculpt to create eye sockets.

Contributors

Michael Adcock is currently studying Computers at the University of Houston. His hobbies include computer games, British comedy & science fiction movies and Television. His proudest accomplishment is having graduated 3rd in his high school class.

Julia Ko is a 9th grade student at University Hill Secondary School in Vancouver, British Columbia. Her other interests are computers and reading. She is most proud of how quickly she designs origami models and wants everyone to know that she designed the model included here while she was bored to death at the Vancouver Opera.

Daniel Stillman is currently a sophomore at City College of the City of New York. Beyond his enjoyment of origami design he is interested in physics, metaphysics and is on a continuous search for "the ultimate spiritual truth."

Daniel E. Moraseski is a 7th grade student at Manalapan-Englishtown Middle School. His interests include maps, math, origami, reading and computers. He also plays drums and is a Boy Scout. He is most proud of having placed 29th in the "National MathCounts junior high competition."

Paul Fischer is in the 11th grade at DeSoto High School in DeSoto Missouri. He enjoys playing the flute and is training to be a carpenter or an architect. When designing origami he enjoys trying to create models which are fairly realistic but simple to fold.

Jimmy Kane is a student at Hammond High School in Columbia, MD. He enjoys hockey and playing pool as well as origami. He was 10 years old when he created his "Spotted Bunny" which was modeled after his pet rabbit "Buster."

Eric Barr lives in Columbia, MD and is a student at Atholton High School. His interests include acting and war gaming. His proudest accomplishment is having played the lead role in "Joseph & the Amazing Technicolor Dreamcoat."

Michael LaFosse has been designing origami for over two decades and is now working full-time as an origami artist and producer. He is also a lover of nature and a gourmet chef. The models included here were created when he was still in his teens.

Julia Einbond is a 10th grade student at Horace Mann High School. Her hobbies include playing flute, tennis and neurobiology. She also does volunteer work reading stories to children at her local public library. She is most proud of having performed a piccolo solo in the "Bryant Park Young Performers Concert Series" in New York.

Aaron Einbond attends Hunter College High School in Crestwood, NY and is in the 12th grade. His hobbies other than origami are composing music, biology, and playing clarinet. His proudest accomplishment is having had a piece of his music performed by a local symphony orchestra. He loves the natural world and enjoys creating origami because it gives him an opportunity to show his admiration of animals.

Troy Elliott is a student at Atholoton High school in Columbia, Maryland. He likes to play the trumpet, work with computers & MIDI musical instruments, as well as do origami and read. He is proud of many of his accomplishments but most proud of his ability to give emotional support to others when they are in trouble.

Kevin Thorne is currently studying wildlife management at the University of Missouri. His interests include origami, music, singing, camping and spelunking. He has 4 brothers and is most proud of having sung a duet with his twin brother at his oldest brother's wedding.

Winson Chan is an engineering student at Simon Fraser University in Vancouver, British Columbia. His interests other than origami include roller blading and computer graphics. He is most proud of his engineering of origami designs which include a 270 unit modular built from a sonobe unit.

Alisdair Post-Quinn is currently taking a year off before going to college. He enjoys music, alpine skiing, frisbee, "DJing" on the radio and at school dances, juggling and computers. He has designed many models and considers his "Balloon Man" to be the simplest.

JC Nolan is a artist / technologist and has been exploring origami design for several years. The early contributions included here, first designed when he was a kid, were designed while doodling around with traditional decorations in one of his favourite origami books.

Marc Kirschenbaum is a college graduate in computer science and works at a job search agency of which he is part owner. His enjoys guitar playing & appreciates a wide variety of musical styles. He also likes to play bridge. His proudest accomplishment is having been selected as a member of the Board of Directors of Origami U.S.A.

Jeremy Shafer is currently in graduate school and has been designing models for may years. He is an accomplished actor, dancer, singer, unicycler and juggler as well as a prolific origami designer. His proudest accomplishments are juggling 9 balls at one time and designing an origami model of a set of nail clippers which actually works!

Eric Anderson is an 11th grade student at MMI Preparatory School in Hazleton, Pennsylvania. He enjoys baseball and baseball cards, comic books, and "Magic: The Gathering" playing cards. He is most proud of having won the "Northeast Pennsylvania Spanish Contest" 2 years in a row.

Gabriel Willow lives in Liberty, Maine. He is home-schooled and will be entering college this coming year. He is a lover of nature and enjoys birding, painting and drawing as well as capturing nature in origami forms. He is most proud of having had his work included in the "Origami by Children" exposition for the last four years and of the fact that he has sighted over 375 species of birds.

Judging Criteria for Origami by Children

Quality of Folding:

Models must be neat, attractive and suitable for exhibition. The winning models will be displayed at the OrigamiUSA Convention in New York City and later will be sent to other locations in the United States, as requested. This can include regional conventions, libraries, and schools, as requested. They will be in circulation for approximately three calendar years.

Please note the following:

- Select a model that you can fold crisply and beautifully. The appearance of the model is more important than its complexity.

- Models should be 5 inches to 10 inches in size.

- Modulars must have STRONG locks (without glue).

- Action models will remain stationary while on display.

Creativity of Presentation:

- Interesting paper selection and or folding techniques can enhance a model's visual appeal

- Choose a weight and or texture of paper appropriate to the model. Practice and experiment with different papers to see how they affect the completed model.

- Models are displayed standing, hanging or mounted on wire or paper. If you have a creative display/technique, please feel free to include it.

Originality:

- Original designs are encouraged, but not required. Credit should be given to original creator.

- Diagrams and books on origami can be found in schools, public libraries or the Internet.

- Original designs will be given special consideration by the judges.

- Age of entrant is also taken into consideration - a beautifully folded simple model by a young child is preferred to a complex one that is not folded as well by an older child.

Entry requirements for Origami by Children

- Entrant must be 18 or younger as of March 31, of participation year.
- Models must be 5 inches to 10 inches in size
- Modular must have very STRONG locks (without glue).
- Entrants must include one completed entry form (in English) for each model. Please print clearly.
- Do **not** draw on, or use glue or tape on model.
- Do **not** use genuine U.S. currency when folding money folds.
- All entries must be received no later than March 31 of participation year.
- There is a limit of two models per entrant. Only one entry will be selected for inclusion in the final judging process.

If any of the above requirements are not met, the entry is disqualified.

All entries become the property of Origami USA. All participants will be informed of their standings in the competition within one month of the judging. The decisions of the selectors are final. Please feel free to copy and share the entry form with your local library, school, recreation or youth centers.

Send all entries to the address listed on the entry form available at www.origamiusa.org/obc.

Origami by Children

Since 1978, OrigamiUSA has sponsored Origami by Children, an annual exhibition of outstanding origami models folded and/or designed by children from around the world. Origami by Children provides an inspiration for children of all ages to explore their own creative potential as well as to enjoy the creativity of other children.

Every year children are invited to submit their best-folded models; either their own creations or the designs of others. The finest of these are selected to become the Origami by Children exhibit for that year. The exhibit is first displayed at the Annual Convention held by OrigamiUSA. Then during the year the exhibit is available to travel to schools and libraries around the USA.

For information on how to participate in Origami by Children, please visit the website of OrigamiUSA at www.origamiusa.org/obc. OrigamiUSA is the national American society devoted to paper folding.

For information on how to join please visit www.origamiusa.org or write to: admin@origamiusa.org or

OrigamiUSA
15 West 77 Street
New York, NY 10024-5192

Made in the USA
Lexington, KY
04 December 2014